Will Ford and Matt Lockett are indeed advancing the God-inspired dream of Rev. Dr. Martin Luther King, Jr. Two paths united beyond skin color come together to bridge the racial divide in this compelling saga, destined to turn the pages of history towards victory.

Dr. Alveda C. King
Evangelist

The lives of Will Ford and Matt Lockett intertwine in such a startling way that it could only have been orchestrated by God! In their book, *The Dream King*, they tell of their healing from personal pain as well as the powerful reconciliation that occurred on behalf of their families and communities. Will and Matt carry a testimony filled with hope for the healing of racism, for the abolishment of abortion, and for the restoration of the world to God's original design. Unity, after all, has always been God's idea.

Bill Johnson
Bethel Church, Redding, CA
Author of *God is Good* and *Hosting the Presence*

They say you can lose yourself in a good story, but it's even better if you can find yourself in one. Matt Lockett and Will Ford have found themselves in a supernatural storyline that spans generations, and they have uncovered startling details from our country's history that are still impacting our lives today. Their message catches us all up in a divine epic that only God could write. Our nation is more divided than ever before, and polarizing extremes threaten to tear away the fabric of our union. Will we repeat the mistakes of the past and suffer the consequences, or will we break the cycle of curses and enter into blessing? What is certain is that we're all in need of healing right now. Matt and Will's lives and the message they carry are a healing balm for our collective soul. For everyone's sake, read this book and live the dream.

Jim Garlow
Pastor, Skyline Church, San Diego, CA
Author of *Well Versed*

I once read that the things that most impact our lives are the books we read and the people we meet. This statement certainly applies to my good friends Matt Lockett and Will Ford and the book that chronicles their story. While *The Dream King* is filled with intricately woven storylines, there is a common thread that runs through all our lives. The King Himself chooses when and where we are born, and these details are all connected to our destinies in Him. Never is this truth more evident than in the remarkable intersection of the lives of these two men. Theirs is a story for the ages, especially this present age.

From hurt to healing, *The Dream King* is filled with hope, history, humility, and heritage. It has the potential to unite this nation in one common bond of unity for the sake of The King and His Kingdom! *The Dream King* goes right to the heart of what ails this nation—division—motivating us to tear down walls and build bridges with the timber of the cross. A must read for this age and all ages!

Elvin Hayes
NBA 50 Greatest Players
Naismith Memorial Basketball Hall of Fame–1990
Entrepreneur/Businessman

In the midst of the present milieu of racial tension and violence in America, God, the beneficent Author of History, has injected an alternate storyline of outrageous hope into our seemingly-fated fractured national soul. In fact, I call it one of the greatest stories ever told: the story of two men, two families, slave owner and slave, two races, made one through a prayer for freedom—An Epistle of Miracles!

Lou Engle
Founder, TheCall
Author of *The Jesus Fast*

Healing the racial divide in America is one of the nation's greatest spiritual needs. Will Ford and Matt Lockett have written a compelling book that is a must-read for believers from every community. This story shows how each one of us can overcome our personal pain and enter into our God-given destiny. Will and Matt were led from their heritage of the classical, oppressive master/slave relationship of their ancestors to a covenant friendship that celebrates their differences. Read, follow, and obey their revelations, because there's hope for each one of us and every community in our nation!

Harry R. Jackson, Jr.
Chief Convener of The Reconciled Church Movement
Pastor, Hope Christian Church, Beltsville, MD

Will Ford and Matt Lockett have written a powerful story that has to be read right now! God is beginning to manifest the dream he gave to the great Civil Rights leader Martin Luther King, Jr. This book does a wonderful job of proving it and teaching you how to also become that dream. Stories embed their cultures within them, and this story will help you to see how our God is just, caring about civil rights even more than we do. God is love, and His love is the only thing that will create a salve over the racial wound of America. I don't know if I have ever been so impacted by a story with so many prophetic details as this one. Both Will and Matt's life journeys have been intricately woven together in a way that shows God Himself slapping racism in the face. Their lives bring forth a revelation to this generation, and their teaching is reformational.

Shawn Bolz
Author of *Translating God, God Secrets, Keys to Heaven's Economy*

The Dream King is a remarkable account of the miraculous intersection of two men's lives in a storyline spanning centuries, written by none other than God Himself. Together Matt and Will have reached back through the pain of shared history to bring God's healing, hope, and redemption to a troubled land. This book will inspire you to participate in fulfilling God's dream for America and to turn the curse of slavery and racial division to a blessing of reconciliation and unity.

Jane Hamon
Pastor, Vision Church @ Christian International
Author of *Dreams and Visions* and *The Deborah Company*

The Dream King is a dynamic revelation of the way God weaves our life stories together. Matt and Will's story reveals how God works steadily and silently during times of our past sorrows and foolish pride; these dark threads are woven in by the Weaver's skillful hand. When the loom is silent and the shuttle ceases to fly, He unrolls our canvas and explains the reason why things happened in our lives.

In the end, the gold and silver threads of our lives shine forth in the pattern God has planned all along. Yes, *The Dream King* is all about the work of our God in the war against our adversary. In the end, the miracle of our Savior is an amazing revelation of God's love for each and every one of His children.

Dennis Lindsay
President and CEO, Christ For The Nations Institute

We are living in the midst of a cultural and spiritual impasse that demands a new paradigm, a new way of thinking. Without this metanoia, we will hopelessly repeat our historical low points and sentence the next generation to more chaos and cultural turmoil. Will Ford and Matt Lockett have given us a masterpiece, a solution from Heaven above. Their improbable story contains the seeds of one of the most powerful reformations that could hit this planet. *The Dream King* is the signature of Heaven for a generation, contained in two lineages played out in the lives of these world shakers. This authentic, courageous, inspiring book will certainly move hearts—and, equally as important, it will move history. I highly recommend this long-needed prophetic treatise!

Sean Smith
Director, Pointblank International
Author of *Prophetic Evangelism* and *I Am Your Sign*

God is the author of creation, and He is writing a story that weaves together our very lives. If you need evidence of God's sovereign direction in the lives of His people, you need to look no further than the book you are holding. *The Dream King* unveils a story of love and racial healing that only God could author. This book will renew your hope and challenge you afresh to believe for racial healing in America. I encourage you to read with your heart wide open to the possibilities of God and wonder at His prophetic poetry in our lives. Will Ford and Matt Lockett are not only dear friends, they are men of God whose character, integrity, and walk with God I admire. I have known these brothers for over a decade and have been personally challenged and encouraged by their stand for righteousness and justice.

Billy Humphrey
Director, International House of Prayer–Atlanta
Co-Founder, OneRace Movement

The Dream King is an intimate look into the spiritual history and divinely intertwined prophetic journeys of Will Ford and Matt Lockett. The astounding stories in this book will increase your faith in the supernatural call of God and challenge you to discover His heart regarding racial reconciliation, justice for the pre-born, and national healing. You will be provoked by their sacrificial obedience to God and inspired by their covenant friendship. Read this book with an expectation for the Sovereign God to invite you into His storyline!

Christina Bennett
Communications Director, Family Institute of Connecticut

Once every century a cultural anomaly appears that challenges the current, controlling zeitgeist. The anomaly, once an outlier, erupts into a generation's consciousness, creating a paradigmatic shift that completely destroys the prevailing injustice. The irreversible result is the redemption of lost years and a transformed future. Will and Matt's relationship, pre-ordained by Providence, personifies this new paradigm that 21st century America so desperately needs. Read every single page in this book. Allow each word to permeate your soul. Be inspired to take action. Their message has the inherent power to be the catalyst that crushes racism once and for all. Matt and Will have initiated us into America's healing moment that may finally realize the prescient dreams of Martin Luther King, Jr.

William J. Ostan, LL.M., J.D., M.P.P.

The Dream King is a gripping, real-life story that will not only convince you that Providence is working in people's lives today, but that it is possible for us to reconcile beyond color barriers. We are all one blood and called to be God's children. Racism has no place in today's world, and Will Ford and Matt Lockett's story needs to be played out between individuals, street-by-street, in every city and place. This book is absolutely life-changing!

Cindy Jacobs
Founder, Generals International
Author of *Possessing the Gates of the Enemy*

The message of *The Dream King* is critical for this hour in history. I can think of no one better than Matt and Will to carry this message of healing, reconciliation, and justice. It has been birthed through them from a deep place of prayer and friendship with God. Their lives and this story are a prophetic sign and declaration that God intends to bring healing to this wounded nation. When their story becomes our story, hope will win the day, and darkness will flee.

Banning Liebscher
Pastor, Jesus Culture, Sacramento, CA
Author of *Jesus Culture* and *Rooted*

THE
DREAM
KING

HOW THE DREAM OF MARTIN LUTHER KING, JR. IS BEING FULFILLED TO HEAL RACISM IN AMERICA

WILL FORD and MATT LOCKETT

N|T NEWTYPE

This book is dedicated to our fathers, William Lawrence Ford, Jr. and Bobby Eugene Lockett, who only knew a small part of this story that spans generations and touches more lives than they could have imagined.

Will and Matt

CONTENTS

ACKNOWLEDGMENTS

Will and Matt would like to thank our families for helping to make us the men that we are. Our wives have been both anchors in stormy seas and wings that have allowed us to fly. Our children have been a constant reminder to always pursue what is best for the next generation. We love you.

We owe a great debt of gratitude to our spiritual family who has provided us inspiration and encouragement throughout the years. Had it not been for our spiritual fathers, Lou Engle and Dutch Sheets, perhaps none of this would have ever happened. The alternative is hard to imagine.

Cindy Jacobs, Alveda King, and Harry Jackson, your unrelenting pursuit of righteousness, justice, and prophetic witness to a generation has inspired us in so many ways. Thank you so much for your friendship and mentorship.

Peggy Scolaro, our editor, has become an irreplaceable addition to the dream team. Thank you for bringing more than skill. You brought heart and soul.

FOREWORD

Whether in a marriage, a friendship, or even a business partnership, it is truly a wonderful thing when the destinies of individuals converge through the providential hand of God. His goodness, wisdom, sovereignty, and foreknowledge can often be seen in the process, and the fruit of such relationships—children, ministries, positive changes on earth—reveal the purposeful nature of our God. Such is the case with Will Ford and Matt Lockett. I have watched *thousands* of people sit in stunned silence as these men share their narrative. Don't be surprised if at times you put the book down and weep as you read this powerful story.

God, *The Dream King,* as Will and Matt refer to Him, places dreams in each of us. The sovereign Creator weaves His plans and purposes into our DNA while we're still in the womb. God then goes to work after we're born, shaping our lives, and leading us toward the fulfillment of His plans for us. At several points along the way, pieces of our destiny will be released through relational connections with others. God-ordained relationships are all about enabling us to fulfill God-given dreams.

When the dreams of Matt Lockett and Will Ford converged, however, it became obvious to all who know them that this alignment was about more than each one helping the other. It was about the two of them helping all of us come more into alignment with God's heart. *The Dream King* had placed *His* dreams in them separately, and, through one of the most amazing convergences you'll ever hear about, fused the two dreams into one. These men are now dreaming God's dream together.

At times, it is astounding to hear the detailed way God has woven together the lives of these two men. In a story that could only be orchestrated by the Divine, I challenge you to begin seeing the way God intends for us to dream and work with Him to see His purposes established in the earth. Let this story stir the dreaming nature of God within you—because you were also meant to run with *The Dream King*.

There are often painful delays in the fulfillment of our dreams. Much of Dr. King's dream is still in process. On a personal level, all of us have private dreams which, as yet, remain unfulfilled. But as Will and Matt help us see, we must never stop dreaming. For when dreaming ends, hope dies.

The book you're holding will change you. I believe it will also be used to change a nation. Read it and dream with Will and Matt ... and yes, with God. Become part of the dream team God is building, and let Him bring forth through you the power to change a nation.

Dutch Sheets
Author of *Intercessory Prayer* and *An Appeal to Heaven*

PREFACE

Will Ford and Matt Lockett have co-written this book to give a stunning example of how people are more connected than they realize. Some consider strange occurrences as mere coincidences, but, as Christians, Will and Matt see the unmistakable work of an unseen God leading and guiding our every step. Providence is the understanding of God's divine leading in our lives, and the authors believe it is God's dream for us to interact and connect in deeper, meaningful ways with each other in unity through diversity. It is for this reason that the authors refer to Jesus Christ, the King of kings, as *The Dream King*.

The goal of this book is to provide a Biblically-based point of view for how to understand, interpret, and connect events and ideas through God's meta-narrative. The story cites scripture throughout as a way of connecting the experiences of the past 400 years in America to the larger storyline of humanity that God is carefully overseeing. Through this lens, readers will begin to see and understand both the tragedy and the triumphs of life in this nation.

The book captures the storyline of each author and is written in the first person. Introducing each section are the words "Will speaking" or "Matt speaking" to help the reader easily identify the point of view being expressed.

In some instances, the authors give details of dreams that are understood to be from God for the purpose of encouragement, insight, and direction. This, too, connects to the book title and points to God as the source of divine information. In most cases, these dreams refer to visions that occurred while the person was asleep. However, dreams may also describe the vision of a person's life—as Dr. Martin Luther King, Jr. articulated in his iconic *I Have A Dream* speech.

Historical documents are cited that reveal not only historical facts but also vividly capture the spirit of the times in which people lived. In particular, this book includes excerpts from *Born in Slavery: Slave Narratives from the Federal Writers' Project, 1936-1938*, a collection of interviews by the Work Projects Administration (WPA) conducted during the presidency of Franklin D. Roosevelt. Dispatched across the United States, interviewers recorded the narratives of former slaves who were still alive at the time. The accounts captured the exact words of surviving African Americans. Their stories appear in their authentic parlance, out of respect for the people who lived during the time of slavery.

When you hang around the Dream King,

you get into a dream stream.

You join yourself to a dream team,

and you do the Martin Luther King thing.

Chapter 1

KETTLE PRAYERS

Will speaking:

Before my father, a successful business man, passed away in 2008, he shared memories with me of being a 5-year-old sharecropper's son, growing up poor in Lake Providence, Louisiana. He chuckled telling me the story of how he washed clothes in a cast iron kettle wash pot. Without washing machines in those days, my father's feet were the agitators. He laughed as he remembered being a little boy, with the kettle full of clothes, lye soap, and water, marching in place, working out the dirt by tromping the clothes with his feet. Of course, neither was there a machine to dry our clothes like we have today, so, with clothespins in hand, he placed everything on a clothesline to dry in the Louisiana wind. Of all his work on the farm, this chore was the highlight of his day. It was his delight.

For my father, William Ford Jr., or "Ned," as he was nicknamed, washing clothes was story time for him as a young boy. As he washed clothes and placed them on the clothesline, his great-grandmother Harriet Locket sang songs and told him stories. Many times she told him how the slaves used the same black kettle pot he was using, too, not just for cooking and washing clothes, but also for prayer. Harriet and her husband Levi Locket came from a long line of Christian slaves who looked to God for salvation and freedom. Little did either of them know back then, a five-year-old boy and his great-grandmother working on a clothesline, that the God of history was working on His own divine storyline involving our family.

In the Bible, Ephesians 2:10 states that we are God's "workmanship in Christ," walking out the works He prepared for us before the foundation of the world. The English word workmanship is translated from the Greek word *poiema*, (pronounced "poy-ay´-muh"). We recognize the word "poem" was derived from *poiema*. Consider the implication of this passage: We are God's poem. We are His dream. Moreover, *poiema* was the word used to describe the work of a skillful and masterful fabric maker. Watching an artistic weaver use different threads to design a garment's tapestry is both fascinating and mysterious. As we watch the artist accomplish the finished product from the backside, the threads appear as tangles, knots, and blotches of colors. It all looks haphazard and chaotic from that point of view, but occasionally the artist turns the poiema around to give us a glimpse of the beautiful tapestry being created. From that perspective, we can see how every stitch and every knot form an integral part of a vast, magnificent plan.

Our perspective on life resembles the reverse side of a great tapestry made by God, our Masterful Artist. The stories of our individual lives are threaded by God into His plan for all of history. Only from the point of view of our Maker is it possible to see how every storyline works together and makes sense when united. For most of our lives, we only focus on the back of God's tapestry, with its loose-fitting threads, jumbled tethers, and contrasting colors. Sometimes God's light shines through the garment of history, and we get a momentary hint of His greater design as He intertwines darker and brighter times, giving us peeks at the transcendent beauty and redemptive meaning of His work in our lives.

God has a tailor-made plan, purpose, and destiny for our lives, woven into the family in which we are born and enmeshed into the nation in which we live. As He skillfully stitches everything together, He starts by connecting us providentially to the storyline of what He has already begun through those who have gone before us. And that is exactly what has happened to me through this kettle and America's history. It's not a coincidence that the kettle comes from my father's family in Lake Providence. As you will see while reading this book, the lake of God's providence is deeper and wider than you might think. Through one of America's darkest stains in history, American slavery, the Light of *Providence* shines forth His redemptive power.

THE HISTORY OF THE KETTLE

Christian slaves on my father's side of the family used a kettle pot for cooking and for washing clothes, but my father was told by his great grandmother Harriet Locket that the kettle was also used for prayer because of the cruelty of their slave master. He was a very wicked slave owner, with an overseer who beat his slaves for any minor offense. For example, a story has been passed down about our great-uncle Willie, who went fishing without asking for permission.

The master decided to use Uncle Willie as an example on the plantation. When Willie returned from fishing, he was tied to a tree. His face, chest and stomach were pressed up against the tree, and his arms and legs were tied together around the other side of it. The slave master then beat Willie with a shredded leather strap containing pieces of rock, glass, and iron, what slaves called back then "the cat of nine tails." This instrument, of course, tore away the skin as Willie was beaten. When his beating was finally over, the skin of his back hung like ribbons, and his torn flesh bled profusely. Family members carefully wrapped his body in a bed sheet smeared with lard or cooking grease to prevent it from sticking to his skin, using it as a giant bandage to stop the flow of blood. However, despite their tender efforts, Willie bled to death during the night.

This same slave master also beat my ancestors for praying. Slaves were not allowed to pray on his plantation. He assumed they were praying for freedom—and he didn't want them even to consider the possibility or hope of freedom. Ironically, he wanted his slaves to be Christians, believing their faith would make them better workers and more committed to him. Part of this strategy lay in what he taught them. He and other slave masters would pervert the gospel and legalistically teach, "If you slaves want to go to Heaven, you better obey your master. That is what this Bible says." While we know the gospel is based on salvation by grace and not works,[1] it was easy to mislead slaves back then because it was against the law for slaves to read or write. Ironically, while their masters wanted their slaves to be Christians, they didn't want them to pray. It was believed that prayer would foster hope, and if their slaves had hope, they would run away. So, if the slave master heard them praying, he would beat them. Nevertheless, these courageous Christian slaves in my family prayed anyway.

In spite of the danger, my enslaved family members would sneak into a barn late at night while everyone else was asleep, making sure their prayer meetings were never seen or heard. As they carefully opened the door, they eased into the barn, carrying the black cast-iron kettle. Once inside, they turned the kettle upside down, so the opening was on the dirt floor of the barn; then they placed rocks under the rim of the kettle to prop it up, creating a narrow opening. They would lie on the ground, prostrate around the kettle, with their mouths close to the opening. The kettle would then muffle their voices as they prayed softly through the night.

One of my family's ancestors who was present in these prayer meetings passed down the story of secret prayer around the kettle. These slaves didn't believe they would ever see freedom in their own lifetimes, so they prayed for the freedom of their children and their children's children. They risked their lives to pray for the freedom of future generations.

One day freedom did come. A young girl who attended those prayer meetings was set free from slavery. This teenaged girl (unfortunately, no one alive today knows her name) saw fit to pass down the cast iron kettle because she knew that she and all those born after her were standing on the sacrifice of others' devotion to Christ. She was careful to preserve and pass on both the kettle and its history. She passed it to Harriet Locket, who passed it to Nora Locket, who passed it to William Ford, Sr., who passed it to William Ford, Jr., who gave it to me, William Ford III.

The 200-year-old cast iron kettle pot handed down through Will Ford's family.

PRAYER BOWLS IN HEAVEN

It is important to understand what took place spiritually as these slaves prayed. Although they were only using the kettle as an acoustic means to keep their prayers from being heard, my family's kettle on earth became a representation of prayer bowls that collect our prayers in heaven. The Bible speaks of "bowls full of incense, which are the prayers of the saints" before the throne of God (Revelation 5:8). Scripture also says that at some future point, no doubt when God determines the time is right, He adds His fire to these prayers (Rev. 8:3-5). Is the incense that

God adds the prayers of the Holy Spirit, who prays with groanings that cannot be uttered (Rom. 8:26)? Do these bowls contain the prayers of all who have gone before us, current Christians around the world, or the prayers of Jesus our great high priest? It could be all of the above. What we do know is that at some point, according to Revelation 8:3-5, these prayers are combined, hurled to Earth, and answered in the form of God's judgments and power.

One of the things released to Earth through these prayers is bold voices. For my ancestors, these bold voices were revivalists and white Christian abolitionists who became voices for the voiceless. They knew any Christian who was a slave was their brother, and they laid their lives down for them. Many abolitionists had their houses burned, were shot, killed, or lynched, because they chose to suffer with the people of God like Moses did with the children of Israel, rather than compromise and wink at slavery. Their storylines were threaded together with their Christian brothers in slavery as they prayed and advocated for their freedom.

What I have realized is that a godly remnant of white abolitionists and Christian slaves prayed into existence the First and Second Great Awakenings. Had it not been for these revivals, slavery would not have ended in America. Because of the prayers of Christian slaves and abolitionists, England and the colonies were shaken when the First Great Awakening took place between 1730 and 1740. That which may have been God's offer of a divine remedy—revival—became divine preparation for the colonists' war for freedom—the Revolutionary War. Colonial America was set free from the British, yet the institution of slavery remained intact. Nevertheless, it was God's intention that everyone be free. The Body of Christ kept praying, and then the thunder of Revelation 8:5 was again poured out. America was rocked by the Second Great Awakening, starting in 1790 and peaking in 1850, as God tipped the bowls of prayer over the nation once more. And, as before, that which could have been the divine remedy—revival—prepared a nation for divine judgment—the Civil War. By the end of the war, President Lincoln spoke of it as God's judgement. In his *Second Inaugural Address* he stated:

> Fondly do we hope, fervently do we pray, that this mighty scourge of war may speedily pass away. Yet, if God wills that it continue until all the wealth piled by the bondsman's two hundred and fifty years of unrequited toil shall be sunk, and until every drop of blood drawn with the lash shall be paid by another drawn with the sword, as was said three thousand years ago, so still it must be said, "The judgments of the Lord are true and righteous altogether."[2]

Finally, the institution that everyone thought would always remain intact was abolished. Merely seven years earlier, in 1857, the *Dred Scott* Supreme Court legal decision had declared that slaves had no rights in court, and many thought this ruling sealed the fate of slavery. Most believed that the issue was settled, but God released a revival to turn hearts, and a Civil War to turn a nation so that slavery would come to an end. Cries in bondage had come up before God's throne as incense. Just as He did for Israel in Egypt, He tipped the bowl of deliverance and ended slavery. Remembering the cries of slaves praying underneath kettles and circuit-riding revivalists and abolitionists,

God raised up reformers like William Wilberforce in England and Frederick Douglass in America. Through them and many others like them, He removed the scarlet thread of slavery from the fabric of our nation.

Each person was adding his or her individual thread as a storyline in God's history, but the history they were making would not be complete without the work of future generations being woven into their own. Scripture speaks of the heroes of faith and proclaims:

And all these, having gained approval through their faith, did not receive what was promised, because God had provided something better for us, so that apart from us they would not be made perfect. (Hebrews 11:39-40)

Many promises made to Abraham and other biblical patriarchs were not fulfilled within their lifetimes. This seems to be contradictory. God made these leaders a promise, yet they personally did not receive the fulfillment. Again, the explanation is simply that God sees the generations as being much more connected than we do. He may promise a person something and bring it to pass through that person's grandchildren. In His mind, doing it through a person's descendants is the same as doing it through the original individual.

Christians of many races throughout American history have understood that freedom is never free. They paid a price, sacrificing their lives for our freedom today. My heart is moved when I remember those like my great-uncle Willie, who was strapped to a tree and beaten to death. I am forever grateful for those who risked their lives to intercede for future generations by praying underneath our family kettle. But, please understand, my heart is even more overwhelmed, knowing that they were not alone. I'm sure that your family has stories, too. How wonderful it is that, in Christ, my stories are your stories, and your stories are mine. Remember, as Christians we share the same heritage.

Our collective history is made from a diverse yet unified remnant—great heroes of faith in America who were passionate for the One who paid the ultimate price for everyone's freedom. Jesus Christ willingly gave His body to be whipped, beaten, and strapped to a tree for us all (see Gal. 3:13-14). He not only risked His life, but He gave His life as a sacrifice so that future generations would be free from the slavery of sin and hell (see Isa. 53:12, Luke 22:37). By accepting His sacrifice as payment for our sins, we become family members who participate in the power of His victorious resurrection (see Rom. 5:6-8; 8:34). As the author and finisher of our faith, by His stripes He is healing history (see Heb. 12:2, 1 Pet. 2:24). Jesus ever lives to make intercession so that you and I, as His family members, can together shape the future with Him (see Heb. 7:25-26, Rom. 8:17). His prayers for unity and promise of greater works beckon us to agree today with what He started in our forefathers yesterday (see John 17:11, 14:12). Through Him, a new remnant is both healing history and making history.

As I meditated on this concept, I thought about the passion God has given me for praying for this nation and the heart He has given me for young people. It dawned on me that to whom much is given, much is required. I realized I not only inherited a kettle as a memorial from the past, I also inherited a calling to pray for revival today that will impact future generations. God is weaving you and me into the power of His yesterday, in order to bring further healing for future generations. Though slavery has ended, it is clear to see the residue of its stain is still on our nation's fabric, and God wants to bring restoration to America. We must allow the power of yesterday to be threaded into our current dilemma, to produce the double portion results we need today. Since 2001, I've carried the kettle around the country holding conferences on prayer, revival, and reconciliation to heal America's wounds.

THE DREAM WEAVER

In addition to the charge to heal the racial issue and start a new justice movement, God gave me a dream about the great dreamer, Dr. Martin Luther King, Jr. Ironically, it was the night before I was to speak at Dr. King's historic church, Dexter Avenue Missionary Baptist Church, in Montgomery, Alabama, where the Civil Rights Movement began. I was there to speak at the request of my dear friend Lou Engle. In the dream, Lou and I were driving in an SUV to the church, but we couldn't get there without picking up Dr. King. As we pulled up to his house, Dr. King came out carrying a white duffle bag with black handles. He went to the curb and dumped out everything in the duffle bag. Once it was empty, to my surprise, he threw away the bag as well. Dr. King then walked over to our vehicle and opened the door to ride with us. In the dream, I thought his bag would make a nice souvenir, but when I went to retrieve it, Dr. King grabbed me and abruptly turned me around. Staring intently into my eyes with his hands on my shoulders, he said: "No! Do not go back and pick that up." He then began to tell me what I needed to do to heal the race issue and contend for justice in America. I began weeping in the dream and woke up with tears streaming down my face.

I knew this dream was important. I shared it with Lou, and he began to tear up as well. I still can't recall what Dr. King said to me, but while praying for the interpretation, I began to understand the significance of the white duffle bag with black handles. Suddenly, I realized the black handles represented my African American race, and the white duffle bag represented my "white baggage." The dream revealed how God wanted me, an African American, to "handle" any unresolved white issues that have been carried for too long.

Honestly, I knew immediately what baggage the Lord was addressing in my dream. I had memories from when I was 13 years old, when a carload full of white teenagers revved their car behind my friends and me as we walked home from a store. As they called us the "N-word," laughed, and followed us, they shouted that they were going to shoot us. We ran, and they chased us, forcing us to run for more than an hour. Another traumatic event happened at 19, when I was falsely accused of shoplifting by a police officer and called "boy" to antagonize me into a verbal and physical altercation. In my 30s, after I moved to a new neighborhood, I was followed and pulled over twice a month for the first three months by the same police officer. I was never speeding; I was just pulled over and released for no reason. It happened often and without any explanation. Those experiences and other stories formed a narrative in my mind regarding police officers and white people from certain areas in my hometown. Over time, subtle traces of bitterness and resentment built up.

In Revelation 12, Satan is identified as the accuser of the brethren. The Greek word for accuser is *kategoros*, which is where we get our English word "category." The diabolical ploy of the enemy is to get us to categorize or stereotype each other, so that we make blanket assessments based on previous experiences before we even begin a conversation with the person in front of us. Negative stereotypes are diabolical categories that destroy people made in God's image, so that we judge them by the color of their skin and not, in the words of Dr. King, "by the content of their character."[3] Whether regionally, ethnically, or by class, stereotypes are baggage that hold grudges, resentments, bitterness, and unforgiveness. After I had this dream, I was able to go to a deeper level of forgiveness for whites and police officers. These suppressed memories had informed and clouded my thinking of others in a way that was deeper than I knew. These thoughts had affected areas of my heart that God wanted to heal.

This change of heart was consistent with anyone who desired involvement with Dr. King's organization in the 1960s. No one could be a part of the movement if he or she had racial hatred or bitterness in his or her heart. The Lord was saying to me, "Empty yourself of any residue of unforgiveness, bitterness, and resentment. Get rid of your white baggage and ride in the new movement that will bring revival and justice to everyone in America." God is speaking to us all through this dream and saying that none of us who are crying out for justice in this hour can get where we're going without picking up the justice mantle that He gave Dr. King, and we cannot get the breakthrough we seek without riding together.

The question before you is the same: What color is your baggage? If you are carrying racial baggage—get rid of it, so we can all ride together in this new justice movement. We need each other. At Dexter Avenue Baptist Church, I shared this dream, and we had a powerful time of repentance and racial reconciliation with hundreds of people in attendance.

After our service, something interesting happened. I had brought with me a book called *A Testament of Hope*, a 700-page book full of speeches and writings by Dr. King. While there, without any page marks or folds to aid it, as the Dream King would have it, I picked up this book, and it suddenly fell open to the *I Have A Dream* speech. Stunned by this, I went to Dr. King's old pulpit and began to read this historic speech as a prayer before the Lord. I was moved to tears when I came to the words, "Let us not seek to satisfy our thirst for freedom by drinking from the cup of bitterness and hatred."[4] This, of course, reminded me of my dream the night before.

King went on to say, "Many of our white brothers, as evidenced by their presence here today, have come to realize that their freedom is inextricably bound to our freedom. This offense we share mounted to storm the battlements of injustice must be carried forth by a bi-racial army. We cannot walk alone"[5] If Dr. King were alive today, I believe he would say a "multi-racial" army.

Later, Dr. King went on to say that he dreamed of the day when, "the sons of former slaves and the sons of former slave owners could sit down together at the table of brotherhood."[6] Little did I know as I read this speech in this historic church, that God was weaving me into this dream and was about to answer a quiet longing of my heart: Who owned our family where this kettle came from? How did these prayers affect their family? Who are they today? Where are they now?

With the inspiration given me from this dream, on January 17, 2005, Lou Engle asked me to speak in Washington DC on Martin Luther King, Jr. Day during a conference he had organized. Since the event was on 1/17, I felt led to speak from Luke 1:17, "I will turn the hearts of the father's back to the children, and the disobedient to the attitude of the righteous." I had no idea all that God had in store for me and my calling to this nation. Little did I know that another important piece of God's tapestry was being woven together. Nevertheless, that's what happened to me and exactly what happened to Matt. Here is his story.

Chapter 2

HIDDEN HISTORY

Matt speaking:

Before I was a missionary, I was in the marketplace. I come from a discipline of telling stories—little stories—actually commercials. It's because of my degree in fine art and my previous career in advertising that I have a great appreciation for filmmaking, especially animated ones. Did you know that traditionally, for every one second of motion in a movie, there are 24 frames of film? You don't notice the individual frames as they go by. All you see is a beloved character stroll across the screen. Maybe you've seen documentaries showing how the old artisans of Disney and Warner Brothers would meticulously hand-craft the intricate details of their animated features, carefully and seamlessly continuing the motion from one frame to the next. Cinematic masterpieces like *Snow White* contain a staggering 166,000 of these individual paintings (more than 2 million sketches and paintings were created in preparation). Original frames from these old animated films are auctioned off today for huge sums of money, each one representing a precious and beautiful piece of art.

An impressive amount of skill, vision, and precision went into each frame to masterfully tell each scene of the story. As the film plays at regular speed, the average person has no idea or appreciation for all that went into it. I have learned that our lives are just like those movies. God is a masterful artist, and He meticulously works frame by frame, designing individual destinies. Unfortunately, many of us just carry on at normal speed, completely oblivious to the involvement of a divine artist in every second of our lives.

God is more involved in the everyday affairs of ordinary people than we realize. King David was in awe of God's attention when he pondered, "What is man, that thou art mindful of him?" (Psalm 8:4). We just go about our average days, traveling at regular speed, never realizing that God is preventing accidents, orchestrating blessings, guiding those around us, involving Himself in national affairs, changing minds, interrupting bad decisions, and turning bad decisions into good choices.

Here we are worried about missing important opportunities, but God is intricately involved in every moment—so involved that He even picks the families we are born into and the moments we arrive. You're here because God inserted you into the story right now. That was His idea. You can rest assured knowing that you're not an accident.

Will's story in the previous chapter gives us a little glimpse into how God predetermines where we will live and the places we will stay. He knows the people we will meet and introduces us to each other in the most unusual ways. As a matter of fact, the Puritans had a word for that: providence.

Nelson's Bible Dictionary defines providence as, "The continuous activity of God in His creation by which He preserves and governs...Through His providence God controls...human birth and destiny...He governs insignificant things and apparent accidents."[1]

You've probably already noticed by now that Will and I share a common name: Lockett (spelled differently). It is so fascinating that Will and I were both providentially born into Lockett families. In my research, I ran across a preface in a book that beautifully describes the intriguing tapestry of God's plan in genealogies:

> The never ending desire, born in most of us to know who we are, from whence we came, even to the n'th degree, drives us, searching into the highways and byways of the past. There is a strange fascination of names repeated here, changed a little there and the continual introduction of the use of surnames for Christian names that thickens the plot, heightens the exigency to forge ahead: until the interwoven mesh of names and families heddles itself into a complete fabric, an ancestral line.[2]

That rather poetic description is actually from a book detailing my personal family history. Until 2013, I never knew it existed, but, as God would have it, I just happened to discover it. As you will soon see, this preface perfectly describes Will's journey and my own.

INTRICATE TAPESTRIES

As Will wrote previously, we are God's workmanship—His

poeima—a masterfully-tailored piece of history perfectly interwoven together according to His divine plan. This fabric of our lives and families creates the backdrop for the nations and the times in which we live. God is in charge of the "interwoven mesh of names"—the weaving of one color in with many others. It all looks like an utter mess from our day-to-day perspective, but when He turns it around, we see the beautiful tapestry He is creating.

Continuing with the theme of *poeima*, I will tell you my part of the tapestry or story of how Will and I met. Keep in mind that God watches over our destinies, watches over our nation, and invites us to shape the future with Him through prayer.

I have been a Christian for most of my life. I accepted Christ at the young age of 15. After college, I pursued a career in marketing and advertising. I was happy raising my family in a local church, where I also served as a youth leader and mentor. Things felt pretty good, but they all came to a screeching halt for me in January of 2004, when my father unexpectedly passed away.

Now, if you have experienced the sudden loss of a parent, you know how it can have the profound effect of throwing you into a tailspin, especially for younger people. Regardless of how healthy your relationship is with your mother or father, things can get turned upside down and shaken when you lose them. Beyond the practical difficulties of making unexpected funeral arrangements and putting their affairs in order, you may go into a period of trying to "figure out your life." That's what happened to me. As a result of those painful experiences, I withdrew from many things—even things that were normally important to me. I not only went through the normal stages of grief, but I also went through a strange discontentment. I now call it "divine discontent" because, in retrospect, I see God was in it. I became very dissatisfied with life-as-usual, even though I excelled in my career. I still received promotions and opportunities in my work, but my heart was nevertheless growing more and more disconnected. What an unexpected thing to go through.

Dad's sudden passing sent me into an extended period of asking big questions that demanded big answers. "Who am I?" "Where did I come from?" "Why am I here?" "What is the story I'm supposed to be telling?" These big questions are not a sign of insecurity, but instead are good things to ask at any stage in life. Your heavenly Father wants you to ask these questions. You see, because I'm a Christian, I believe that things have meaning instead of being utterly random. Your life has meaning, so it's important to take stock of where you are at important milestones and all along the way for that matter.

When you lose the patriarch or the matriarch of a family, something monumental happens. You become the steward of the storyline. The responsibility now falls on you to try to understand what has happened in the past and to decide which direction things will go next. In which way will you point the next generation? Will you repeat the familiar mistakes that have hounded your family for as long as you can remember, or will you break those old destructive patterns? It's a lot to think about, but God is in it.

DIGGING INTO THE PAST

Have you ever researched your family genealogy? I never had, but it was during that time that I determined to try to figure out a big mystery. I knew that a personal frustration of my father's was that very little knowledge existed about our family history. When I was younger, I remember being told that other relatives had run into dead ends in research due to things like courthouse fires, which caused the loss of vital paper records. In fact, I knew nothing of the lineage beyond my dad's grandfather. Somewhere along the way, the story became lost. Records ceased to exist, and the oral history had failed. Sure, there were anecdotes here and there, but no clear picture could be seen or put together. Dots couldn't connect.

In spite of these challenges, I became determined in the days after the funeral to figure out my family tree. I knew from the outset that it would likely be a big one. You see, I come from a small family—just my older brother and I—but my dad was one of 16 siblings (actually there were 17, but one sister died when she was only six months old). My dad used to joke that the large family was because his dad needed labor to work their tobacco farm in Kentucky. I wanted to discover something with substance, but by the end of the summer, I had run into the same roadblocks as everyone else in the past. By August of that year, I was more frustrated than ever before after making no progress. In hindsight, I see that it was right at that tangled mess that God was about to give me a peek at my destiny—a story woven together that I could never have imagined.

It was September of 2004. In the midst of my frustration, I had a dream while I slept one night. That dream seemed completely unrelated to my family research, which had dominated my thoughts. In fact, it didn't seem related to any of my normal experiences. I wasn't a dreamer per se back then, but that dream felt so profound to me. I have now learned that eating late-night pizza gets way too much credit for unusual dreams and that God loves to speak to us in this way. That dream gave me a picture of the extraordinary power of prayer and would go on to completely change my life. I'll go into greater detail about the actual dream in Chapter 4, but for now let me tell you an important element of it. In the dream, I met a man who was praying intensely with young people, and I knew his name to be Lou Engle. At that time, I didn't know Lou Engle.

I didn't understand why I had that strange dream. It was unlike anything I had experienced before, and thoughts of it wouldn't leave me. In the days that followed, it was the last thing I thought about when I went to bed and the first thing I thought about the next day. It stayed with me all day every day for a couple of weeks. Finally, I told the dream to my wife, and by that time I had found out a little more about this man named Lou Engle. I said to my wife Kim, "I think I'm supposed to do something with this."

Let me just say here that you should pay close attention to your dreams. When you're asleep, the Holy Spirit can get past all your intellectual defenses and personal hang-ups. Impossible things can happen in your dreams, and often they are windows to your calling. Dreams are God's invitations into your destiny. Borrowing an idea from Mark Rutland's book *Dream*, I like to say it this way, "I had a dream, but the dream had me." It's for this reason I refer to God as The Dream King.

"Maybe I'm supposed to contact him," I said to my wife. "Maybe this is something for him. I'll just tell him the dream, and then I can be done with this." Famous last words! All these years later, I'm still not done with that dream. At that point, I was just getting started.

Through a few connections with various colleagues, I was able to get in contact with someone who worked with Mr. Engle. I called him and introduced myself saying, "I don't know you, and you don't know me, but I had a dream." To my surprise, he responded, "Oh really? What was your dream?" I hadn't expected him to take me so seriously. I told him the dream, and to my astonishment, he said, "That is very interesting. You dreamed exactly what God has just sent us to do in Washington, DC." As you can imagine, I was stunned. He went on, "We are going to do a conference in January (2005). I think you should come because God might have something for you there."

HEARING YOUR NAME CALLED

Before I decided to go to the conference, I thought I'd learn more about what Lou Engle was doing. During that time, I received a recording of him preaching in which he talked about how Moses turned aside to see the burning bush in Exodus 3:2-4. What stuck out most to me was when he mentioned how Moses heard his name being called by God when he responded to the strange sign. I remember a specific phrase Lou made that deeply impacted me. He said:

What moves you? What is your passion? Stay close to the burning bush in your life. What burns in you and never goes out? When you find something like that, draw close to it, and you'll hear your name called.

Those words pierced my heart, and I decided to draw closer to this situation and attend this conference in DC. That moment reminds me of an Elizabeth Barrett Browning poem, in which she writes:

Earth's crammed with heaven,
And every common bush afire with God:
But only he who sees, takes off his shoes,
The rest sit round it, and pluck blackberries.[3]

In his book *Windows of the Soul*, Ken Gire responds to this poem with a prayer:

Thank You, God,
For Your hand that reaches to me,
touching my arm, tapping my shoulder,
telling me to pause and to look and to listen
at all the windows of the soul.
Help me to see something in those windows,
something of heaven in every earthly event,
something of the divine spark in every human soul.
Please, dear God, give me grace to stand shoes in hand,
before all that in some way bears Your glory,
for I don't want to spend my days
just sitting around
plucking blackberries...[4]

I agree with Gire. I don't want a mundane existence of merely picking the blackberries of this life. I want my eyes to be open to the burning bush encounters all around me so that I can recognize God in each moment. What I have learned is that most of the time coincidences are, in reality, burning bush encounters. God invites us to slow down and ponder what He's working on frame-by-frame in our lives and our nations. If you draw close in these moments as Moses did, you're likely to hear your name being called.

From that time until the January conference, I had only one heart-felt prayer: "God, I want to hear my name called!" I had spent almost an entire year trying to discover something new about who I was. I wrestled through a divine discontent with life-as-usual. I wanted to hear my name called in a holy moment.

I arrived in Washington, DC, and the conference began on January 17, 2005. My wife was unable to travel with me because she was eight months pregnant with our youngest child, so I decided to take my 10-year-old daughter Taylor with me on the journey. Now that I think of it, even her name was a sign to me that God was "tailoring" something special—the *poeima*.

That day, I felt like a raw nerve and an emotional mess. It had been exactly one year to the day since my father had passed away. It concluded a painful and frustrating year for me. That day turned out to be quite a surprise for me since I had never been to a conference like this before. It began with an outdoor prayer meeting at the Lincoln Memorial, which seemed crazy to me. Why would anyone want to do a prayer meeting outside when the wind chill was below zero? Not only that, but the prayer meeting lasted for several hours. Exactly what had I gotten myself into?

I felt a little bit like a spectator that day. I didn't understand what all was going on, but I listened carefully and took a lot of pictures. I'm glad I did because, looking back, I have several photos of Will Ford participating in the gathering, even though I had no idea who he was at the time. It was there that I first heard him share his heart, and I got to join with him in prayer.

Isn't that interesting? God gave me a dream that led me to the steps of the Lincoln Memorial. At the same time, Will came to that very same spot because of a dream. It was the place where Dr. Martin Luther King, Jr. gave his famous *I Have A Dream* speech, and it also just happened to be on Martin Luther King, Jr. Day. Coincidence? We think not.

After a long day in the cold, the conference continued at a local church that evening. My daughter and I went in spite of the fact that we were exhausted from the day. If you have traveled with children, you know how difficult that can be. I'm so glad that we did because that night a man named Will Ford spoke. He brought out onto the platform the kettle that had been handed down from his slave ancestors, and he told the story that you just read about in the previous chapter.

As I said, my emotions were overwhelmed that day. As I listened to the story of the kettle and the slaves who prayed under it, I began to weep. After a year of searching, I had uncovered no significant information about my family, but Will was sharing about his rich spiritual heritage. Suddenly, Will shared a detail about the story that instantly stunned me. He told of how the kettle had been handed down to Harriett Locket, who handed it down to her daughter Nora Locket, who then handed it down to William Ford, Sr., to William Ford, Jr., to William Ford III"— the person standing on the stage.

Just then, my young daughter turned to me and said, "Dad, he just said our name." Remember that leading up to this conference I had been praying only one prayer: "God, I want to hear my name called." Who knew that God would be so literal with His answer to that prayer?

As I sat there overwhelmed, I had an encounter with the Lord in what I can only describe as what seemed like a vision. It was in my mind's eye, but I could see it so clearly. The Lord reached down, pointing at the kettle, and said, "I'm grafting you into this family tree. I'm calling you to be an intercessor for America." That moment changed my life forever.

Afterwards, I spoke with Will at the altar of the church. When I introduced myself, he asked about my last name, "How do you spell it? With one 't' or two?" Our Locketts spelled it with two "t's," but his family had spelled it with only one. Then he asked, "Where are your Locketts from?" I said, "Well, as far as I know, we're from Kentucky." He responded, "Oh, our Lockets were from Louisiana." We both just kind of shrugged and thought it was a strange coincidence, but Will and I prayed together that evening. We repented for sins committed by our ancestors. We also prayed to break generational curses related to racism and division in the nation and released forgiveness. What a precious beginning this was to our extraordinary relationship.

Will and I stayed in contact with each other beyond that event, and we felt a great connection in friendship and as Christian brothers. As our relationship grew, so did our trust and affection for one another and each other's families. What a joy it has been to partner in ministry for many years and to do life together with the aim of just loving each other well.

BIG CHANGES AHEAD

After being there, I also felt connected to Lou Engle and the work he was doing in Washington, DC. It turned out the dream that I had still had a hold on me. I sensed the Lord was strategically changing the way I usually thought about things, and He was pointing me in a new direction. I was determined to continue drawing closer to this burning bush in my life.

A few months later, when my wife could travel again, I returned with her to DC. We were able to visit the ministry base Lou Engle had started, and we spent a weekend with him and his other leaders. We shared stories and dreams with each other, and at the end of the weekend, we all agreed that God was doing something unique. At that time, there was no room or opportunity to join in what was going on there, and, besides, I had to get back to my job and life-as-usual. As you will see in the next chapter, life-as-usual was about to drastically change, and Mr. *Poeima* was about to reveal more of His handiwork in my life.

Chapter 3

POETRY OR PROPHECY?

Matt speaking:

One of our favorite quotes is from William Temple, one of the archbishops of Canterbury, who once said, "When I pray, the coincidences happen. When I don't, they don't."[1] Simply put, we begin to recognize the hand of the Dream King as He answers our prayers. In this chapter, you will see how He not only revealed how He answered our prayers but also the prayers of our forefathers. Also, you will see how after years of ministry work in Washington DC, God revealed the hidden history I longed to know about my family. As Will and I have come to understand, there was more to our introduction on Martin Luther King, Jr. Day than we could have imagined.

GOING FOR BROKE

As part of chasing the dream from God, I had spent a little time with Lou Engle and his team in Washington, DC. I think going back to work the following Monday after visiting the Justice House of Prayer was probably one of the hardest things I have ever had to do. I felt like big changes were coming, but at that moment all I could do was pray for understanding and the Lord's perfect timing. It was only a couple months later that I received an unexpected phone call from Lou. The ministry staff had changed, and Lou made a passionate appeal for my wife and me to help him with the Justice House of Prayer. It was kind of funny because it wasn't much of a pitch at all. Lou said to me, "Hey, I have an idea. Why don't you quit your job, go for broke, and move out here and help me with this thing?" That was it. At that time, we lived in Denver, CO, so he was literally asking us to move across the country. I said, "Well, let me talk to my wife first." I immediately called my wife Kim, who at the time was stuck in traffic somewhere in the city, and I told her what Lou had just asked us to do. It's not an exaggeration to say that we had 20 really good reasons why we couldn't do it.

Think of the inconvenience and the ridiculousness of that proposal. There are always at least 20 reasons why you can't follow God when divine opportunities open up before you, but God often calls us to step forward into those uncharted moments of faith in spite of them all. Would we respond to the burning bush or not?

After we talked back and forth for some time, I asked my wife the concluding question, "Do you think we can do this?" My wife unexpectedly began to laugh and respond unusually. Right at the exact moment that I had asked the question, a passing car suddenly cut her off in traffic and stopped right in front of her. It had a custom license plate that read, "GO DC." That was the message staring her in the face. I'm really glad God told her, so I didn't have to.

Some people laugh at that part of the story, but most people gasp. It's a small detail, but it forces you to think of The Dream King watching over every frame of every second of your life. You can see God as the Author carefully crafting a story with precision. You have to take off your proverbial shoes for something like that. Ponder this for a moment: Where did that person in the other car come from, and what were the circumstances in his life that led him to get *that* license plate? What were the events of that particular day that led him to that specific spot at that exact moment? For a brief moment, his story wove into our story, and my wife got the vital message that was needed. It was either God or a really bad joke.

Believe it or not, my wife responded, "I think we can do it." We had confidence to move forward, and I left a successful career for the unknown. God called me to be a full-time missionary serving in Washington, D.C. with the Justice House of Prayer on Capitol Hill. The days ahead would take me deep into God's heart about national issues, and my relationship with Will would become a pivotal element to walking out my calling and assignment as an intercessor for America.

We moved to the nation's capital and immersed ourselves in prayer for many years, but God did not forget my desire to know about my family history.

THE LAST SHOT

Fast forward to several years later. At that time, Lou Engle lived across the country, and I received a phone call from him because he was planning a large prayer gathering in Virginia. He strongly felt that we should first go to pray at the place

55

where Confederate General Robert E. Lee surrendered to Union General Ulysses S. Grant, marking the end of the Civil War at a place called Appomattox Court House. We felt it was important to pray there in advance of the event because of a dream from God that spoke specifically about Appomattox Court House. It is a dream that has defined many years of our prayers for America, and I will explain the significance of it in Chapter 4. We drove several hours to the place of the surrender, and we stood inside the McLean farmhouse, which has been preserved for its historical significance. There we prayed for revival in America and for our nation, which is divided in so many ways today.

As we left, we stopped by the visitors center of the historic site. Lou and I just happened to stand side-by-side at a small bookshelf, and he picked up the first book that caught his eye. As he opened it, the book fell open to a particular page. Lou blurted out, "Whoa! What's this?" The page was titled, "The Last Shot: The Battle of Lockett's Farm." I had no idea what it was about, but it suddenly felt like I was in another burning bush holy moment as I heard my name literally called once again, just as it had been years before. I bought that book and began to research the topic.

I learned from my study that General Lee and his troops were forced to make a hasty retreat from the Richmond-Petersburg area when the Union army broke through the defenses. The Confederates made a fast-paced march across the middle of Virginia with the hopes of reaching a place to resupply, since their ammunition and resources were quickly running out. Lee's retreat had brought him to a place called Sailor's Creek, which was just before Appomattox Court House. Intense battles

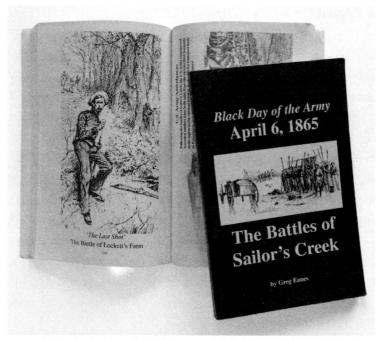

The book taken from the shelf that revealed the history of April 6, 1865.

were fought there on April 6, 1865, and the final battle of the day occurred on a farm owned by a family named Lockett. In fact, Lee's last battle of the American Civil War happened in the front yard of the Lockett house. Three days later he surrendered at nearby Appomattox Court House on April 9. Take a moment to think about this: The American Civil War ended in the front yard of a family with the same uncommon last name as mine. From a spiritual point of view, it seemed like it could be just a coincidence. I was to find out it was so much more than I could have imagined.

A FAMILY TREE REDISCOVERED

About that time, my brother Bob, who had been using gene-alogy tools to do his own research, contacted me. He had finally gotten the breakthrough in our family tree that connected dots we had never before seen put together. In fact, at that time he had traced our family history all the way back to the year 1645. "We came in as settlers through Virginia," he began to tell me. "Virginia? Have I got a story for you," I responded. I began to tell him the curious story of where the Civil War had ended, when he interrupted me, asking, "That's not that place near Sailor's Creek, is it?"

Already I was beginning to tremble. "That's exactly where it is," I said. I sank into my seat as my brother began to explain to me that he had just found records of that property in his research. After a pause which seemed to last forever, he said, "That was our family."

The Battle of Lockett's Farm was not just another random story, coincidentally bearing my last name. It was literally *my* family heritage. To my knowledge, no one in recent generations of our family has known this. It was lost history. Imagine my shock when I learned that the American Civil War ended in my family's front yard. This development was almost more than I could comprehend, and yet I felt there was still more to discover.

I decided to try to find the exact location where the Battle of Lockett's Farm took place. I reviewed old Civil War maps and carefully compared them to modern satellite images. Surprisingly, not much had changed in those rural areas. When I visited the Sailor's Creek battlefield visitor center, I found one of the walls there chronicled the details of the Lockett farm site. I introduced myself to an employee there, and we talked for a while about the land's historical significance. Then he said to me, "You should go over there. I bet Jimmy will show the place to you." I replied, "Jimmy? What place?" You see, I had assumed it was all long gone by now, but I was wrong. He said to me, "The house is still standing. It has been preserved."

Nearby we found the Lockett farmhouse sitting atop a rolling Virginia hillside. A stone memorial stands in the front yard inscribed with the words, "Here Lee fought his last battle." The homeowner graciously allowed my team and me to come inside, and I stood shocked when I saw the Lockett family tree framed and hanging on the living room wall. Beginning with Thomas Lockett in 1645, the genealogy matched my brother's research exactly. It was a very surreal moment. It was my family. Jimmy talked about how different Lockett family members had branched out from that original homestead area. He mentioned how some had gone to Kentucky, which was my line. Others had gone various places, including the deep South, where they were a part of significant historical events.

Historical marker where General Robert E. Lee fought his last battle.

I was left speechless when he then said to me, "Some left here, and went to Louisiana. In some cases, the spelling of the name got changed slightly. For instance, in some cases they had dropped one of the t's at the end of Lockett, likely because of clerical errors in census notes." When that was said, my mind immediately went back to my conversation with Will when we first met on January 17th, 2005. Remember, his family had spelled the name with only one t. What I found myself thinking couldn't possibly be true though, could it? Could there be a direct connection in my family to Will Ford and the kettle? It wasn't uncommon for slaves to take the last names of their owners, so it wasn't out of the question.

I followed up that trip to Lockett's Farm with a visit to Will and his family in Dallas. We laid out all the historical details we had found thus far, and we stared at them, completely overwhelmed. On the one hand, the level of detail and providence of a connection in our families seemed improbable if not impossible. And yet, at the same time, should we have been all that surprised by such an intricate level of detail when we consider a God who is the king of dreams? That convergence was a collective burning bush moment for both Will and me. We looked at each other with tears in our eyes, sensing the holiness of the handiwork of God. Not in skepticism or disbelief, but, in awe, we waited. For months we pondered, "What if?"

HANDIWORK REVEALED

Will and I are similar in that we're both researchers by nature, and we dislike unnecessary embellishment. What we have found, however, requires no exaggeration. After much research, we have discovered that it was my Lockett family who had owned Will's Locket slave ancestors, who were praying for freedom under that cast iron kettle pot.

Let me attempt to sum up the story to this point. My African American friend Will and I were both led by dreams from God to the same spot on the same day—the place where Dr. Martin Luther King, Jr. gave the *I Have a Dream* speech. It was at the Lincoln Memorial, which stands as a monument to the great emancipator who led the nation during a time of unprecedented division and bloodshed in America. The Lord had drawn our attention to the history of Appomattox Court House, where the American Civil War ended, through a dream that gave us vivid language for our prayers. After many years of praying into that dream, I discovered that the last battle of the Civil War, which was fought to end the injustice of slavery, took place in my family's front yard. Will had already been preaching for years with the kettle about the legacy of prayer for abolition. Then, my family was revealed to be the ones who owned those praying slaves. As they were praying for slavery to end, it was as though God drew a line on the land that represented their bondage. When the war got to that line on Lockett's Farm, it could go no further.

Will and I have bound ourselves together as brothers for years, contending for revival in the land, racial healing, and the ending of the ongoing injustice in America. We now realize that God had a much bigger plan in mind, and it was a plan that began long ago.

Will speaking:

The first link that connected my slave forefathers in Louisiana to slave owners in Matt's family in Virginia was an ancestor who appeared in the 1870 census. My oldest known family member in Lake Providence, Louisiana, was named Isaac Locket. He appeared in the 1870 census—five years after slavery ended—when he was 90 years old. In that census, though he lived on Sutton Plantation in Lake Providence, Louisiana, he reported that he was originally from Virginia.[2] In those days, it was common for slaves to be given the last name of the people who owned them. It appears he had been willed off as property to a family member or friend and ended up working the land in Lake Providence. This connection was key, because the Locketts in Virginia were a part of Matt's family tree. They were a very large family and well established in Virginia. In fact, one historical account referred to them enduring as the last great land owners in the state.

After more than a year of additional research, we found even more connections, and we are certain through the evidence we have found that Matt's Lockett family owned my slave forefathers, who prayed for freedom under that kettle pot. You can only imagine my reaction to all of this as it unfolded. I was overwhelmed that God answered my prayers of knowing who had owned those kettle prayer warriors and how our history was connected. To know that I shared this kind of history with one of my best friends left me beside myself. Our families have wept together, reflecting on the redemptive power of God's providential hand.

Matt and I learned another amazing fact about the Lockett family that originated in Virginia. Napoleon Lockett married his first cousin Mary and moved from the family's Virginia homestead to Marion, Alabama. They had 11 children, were very wealthy, and owned hundreds of slaves. Napoleon was an attorney, a planter, and Colonel for the Confederate Army.

Mary, his wife, was a socialite, and she didn't like the fact that the Confederacy didn't have its own flag. She commissioned an artist to design the very first Confederate flag, called the "Stars and Bars." Mary Lockett hand-sewed the flag in her house and then personally delivered it to her friend Jefferson Davis, the Confederate President. In other words, Mary Lockett was the "Betsy Ross" for the Confederacy.

Remember, General Lee's last battle before unconditional surrender at Appomattox Court House was at the Lockett's Farm, part of the family homestead where Napoleon and Mary Lockett lived before moving to Alabama and eventually creating the Confederate flag. Because God answered the muffled prayers of Lockett slaves along with the prayers of white abolitionists, through the same family line that raised up the flag of rebellion in America, the flag of surrender went up on their land in Virginia. Even more beautiful is the fact that, because He is the God of the past, present, and future, He connected two more Christians—again black and white—from the same Lockett family line to war against injustice in our day and to cry out for awakening in our time. He is still writing a redemptive story for us all today.

MORE THAN POETRY

Matt and I were both led by dreams to meet at a prayer gathering on Martin Luther King, Jr. Day, which was held at the Lincoln Memorial where Dr. King said in his famous speech, "I have a dream…that one day the sons of former slaves and the sons of former slave owners will be able to sit down together at the table of brotherhood."[3] Perhaps the *I Have A Dream* speech wasn't just poetry. Maybe it was prophecy. We believe what God has done in our lives is proof that God is still answering the prayer of His Son, the Dream King, better known as the King of kings, who prayed in John 17 that we would be one, and that God's glory would come so the world would believe.

We have also learned that God was answering more than just my slave forefathers' prayers for freedom. He was also moved to answer the prayers from some of Matt's forefathers on the other side of slave history. For example, there was a countercultural abolitionist preacher who took a strong stand against slavery. As you read, we will also reveal Lockett family members who taught former slaves to read and write. You will learn the hidden history of Christian slaves in America, and the other ways God

Matt Lockett and Will Ford leading prayer together.

used them in secret prayer meetings which ended the Civil War at Lockett's Farm.

Matt and I are awestruck by the intricate story that God is writing. He is carefully working frame-by-frame in our lives, and He has joined Matt and me together to war against injustice and to cry out for awakening in our generation. We invite you to slow down and appreciate His workmanship. No doubt, he has prepared good works in advance for you, too. We all are part of this beautiful tapestry, and we long for God's glory to come.

As we go further, you will see that the story only continues to deepen. In the next chapter, we reveal a very important thread in the tapestry that connects us. Through it, God's guiding hand becomes more and more apparent. Thinking about the kettle pot that muffled the prayers of Christian slaves back in Lake Providence, Louisiana, has helped us see that the lake of God's providence is deeper and wider than we know, and that no one is a mistake.

Chapter 4

NO ONE IS AN ACCIDENT

Matt speaking:

After hearing Will and me tell our story, most people say, "Only God could have orchestrated this." We couldn't agree more. When God gets this detailed in revealing a storyline, it's hard to deny His supernatural signs. When you see His divine signposts, they make you stop and ponder. One question we've been wondering is: "Why was this story hidden from us until now?" Will and I have to believe that God waited to reveal our shared history, knowing that it would have maximum impact on the racial tension and unrest our nation is facing right now. Another key question has been, "What is God saying to us all in this?" While we don't have all the answers yet, we are convinced He is revealing that life is precious; nothing "just happens," and no one is a mistake.

I have been involved with various aspects of youth ministry for many years. Although the Millennial Generation (born mid-1980s to mid-2000) has grown up in a uniquely affirming environment, one thing I have heard surprisingly often from these young people is the notion that their lives are an accident or a mistake. I don't mean the cosmic kind resulting from a Big Bang, although that cultural mindset certainly fuels it. This harmful idea comes right out of the individual's experiences. For some, the impression of their accidental existence was carelessly planted by their parents. I believe we can trace the origin of this persistent mindset.

My generation was called Generation X or simply Gen-X (born mid-1960s to mid-1980s). Collectively, we grew up as the products of broken homes and the advent of no-fault divorce. I had childhood friends living in single-parent families who were told that they were an accident in some form or another. Their existence was the inadvertent by-product of the sexual liberation that had defined our parent's generation. They didn't come from planned or wanted pregnancies. They just happened. That thought is a horrible thing to communicate to a child. Psychologists agree that core attitudes about life are formed by around the age of five. Imagine growing up with the mental wound that you're not supposed to be here. Perhaps you're reading this now and thinking, "That was me!"

A SHOCKING PARALLEL: AMERICA'S SCARLET THREADS

It is no coincidence that the tragic court case *Roe v. Wade* became the law of the land right in the middle of a cultural crisis in 1973. America has been down a similar road before with efforts and language designed to dehumanize, marginalize, and disenfranchise a people group—namely Africans and their descendants in America. If we look back in history, we can trace the roots of the ideology of abortion.

A generation of young Americans are growing up today with no knowledge of the insidious agenda that formed the social foundation of the abortion industry. Admittedly, I didn't know anything about it either, but that all changed when God began to direct my attention to it. The first time I understood the abortion issue from an African American perspective is when I heard Will speak at the conference when we met in 2005. In those earliest moments of our connection, God revealed the scarlet thread of abortion that would weave throughout our profound story. Will's path of discovery has given me a lot of understanding and application, especially when I view his experiences in the light of major dreams God has given me about America. I'll discuss those dreams later in this chapter.

Will speaking:

Interestingly, as Matt and I were writing this chapter of the book, dehumanizing images emerged of African Americans, past and present, that outraged many leaders in the Black community. NBA star Lebron James called out a major clothing store for comparing African Americans to monkeys. Also, Hip Hop mogul Jay Z produced a music video confronting dehumanizing and derogatory imagery of African Americans in cartoons, which also portrayed African Americans as primates. Historically, Black leaders have fought often against derogatory portrayals and comparisons of being mere beasts, void of relevance or value. Very few know where this racist mindset originated, however, and its systemic impact within our nation today. This all begs the question: How did this mindset begin?

The underlying influence where this began is with eugenics, which is merely a sophisticated name for racism. Eugenicists believe that food supplies grow arithmetically, and populations grow geometrically. Their plan is for their so-called positive "fit" eugenic desirables to breed and proliferate, while those they classify as negative or "inferior" dysgenic undesirables get weeded out of society, so that the "unfit" do not deplete the resources of the so-called "fit." Francis Galton, a cousin of Charles Darwin, is credited with coining the term, and supported positive eugenics, while others like John Malthus and Charles Davenport began promoting negative eugenics to weed out those they deemed unfit. Eugenicists believe the fallacy that not only is skin color hereditary, but so also is poverty. In other words, they think poverty is inherent, passed on to succeeding generations as a biological trait. Unfortunately, they also believed criminality and intelligence were biologically inherited.

THE SCARLET THREAD OF EUGENICS

What does this have to do with Jay Z, Lebron James, and other celebrities' outrage over dehumanizing imagery of African Americans? During the time period just after slavery, scientists, influenced by eugenics, began to say that people of African descent were closer to apes and monkeys on the evolutionary scale. For example, in "The Basis of Social Relations: A Study in Ethnic Psychology," published by G.P. Putnam's Sons in New York and London as part of the *Webster Collection of Social Anthropology*, author Daniel Brinton claimed that Africans were "midway between the Orangutan and the European white." He added, "The African black presents many peculiarities which are termed 'pithecoid' or ape-like."[1] During this time, Blacks were deemed inferior to whites and were considered the dregs of society. One horrific display of this eugenic mindset was the treatment of an African man named Ota Benga.

Author Madison Grant was one of the co-founders of the American Eugenics Society and an officer of the New York Zoological Society. In 1906, he authorized an exhibit at the Bronx Zoo in which a 22-year-old African named Ota Benga was kept in a cage and displayed in the monkey house. Sharing the cage with Benga was an orangutan. A local Black clergyman who protested the exhibit complained it was intended to be a demonstration of Darwin's theory of evolution. Proponents of Darwinism apparently agreed and labeled the display educational.

During this period, Blacks were considered the lowest form of human development and were considered monkeys and apes by Social Darwinists and other elites in the eugenics movement, whose influence and ideology were invading the sciences and arts. From Blacks being called "porch monkeys" to cartoons portraying Negros with ape-like depictions, as mentioned earlier, African Americans fought against this imagery, knowing that dehumanization leads to elimination through marginalization.

Pamela Newkirk, author of *Spectacle: The Astonishing Life of Ota Benga*, writes:

Indeed, it was a callous disregard for Benga's humanity that resulted in him being exhibited at the zoo. Benga was first brought to the United States by Samuel Verner, an avowed white supremacist from South Carolina and former African missionary. Two years earlier, he had been commissioned by organizers of the St. Louis World's Fair as a special agent to bring back so-called "pygmies"—the diminutive forest-dwellers from Central Africa who some scientists at the time inaccurately considered examples of the lowest form of human development.[2]

It was reported that in one weekend, over 40,000 people came to the Bronx Zoo to see Ota Benga. He was considered nothing more than a pet monkey in a twisted social science project. Ota Benga, distraught and depressed from his treatment, committed suicide by shooting himself in the heart. Eventually, dehumanization through eugenics became a slippery slope leading to the further marginalization of African Americans.

Ota Benga, Bronx Zoo, 1906. Photo: Library of Congress[A]

Eventually, terms like, "imbecile," "moron," and "misfit" became code language for races the eugenicists deemed less desirable. It is hard to imagine today, but it was during this same time in history that eugenic sterilization laws were enacted in 33 states in America to control the population of those deemed genetically undesirable, initially focusing on poor whites, and eventually solely on ethnic minorities. Eugenic medical boards in many cases decided whether people should be sterilized on the basis of being deemed misfits, morons, or imbeciles, and in most cases, these were code terms for people who were African American. Many times these individuals were sterilized against their will or knowledge, as in the case of one victimized African American woman named Elaine Riddick.

When she was 13 years old, Riddick was raped and became pregnant. Later in life, after having problems conceiving, she learned that North Carolina's Eugenics Board had deemed her an imbecile and moron, unfit to birth any more children. Her grandmother, who couldn't read, had been deceived into signing sterilization papers while Elaine was giving birth to her son in the hospital. As reported by *MSNBC*'s investigative news story, moments after she delivered her baby, doctors sterilized her without her knowledge. Today, the woman labeled an "imbecile" by North Carolina's Eugenics Board is a college nursing school graduate, the proud mother of a son who is a college graduate himself and a successful entrepreneur. Sadly, this amazing mother was robbed of the opportunity to bear more children. Seeing the outcome of her son, society was robbed as well. In all, approximately 7,600 poor whites and mostly African Americans were mandated to be sterilized in North Carolina from 1919 to 1977. Finally, the last North Carolina sterilization law was repealed in 2003.[3] C. J. Gamble, an heir to the Proctor and Gamble fortune, was the founder of the Eugenics Board of North Carolina and is connected to a very key figure in the eugenics movement: Margaret Sanger.

THE SCARLET THREAD OF ABORTION

Gamble gave significant monetary support to Margaret Sanger and was also on the board of her organization, The American Birth Control League, which became Planned Parenthood. Planned Parenthood has tried to clean up Sanger's image and deny the racist and eugenic underpinnings of their organization, but according to noted historian Edwin Black, Sanger was definitely part of the eugenics movement and had her own issues with class and race. Though Black speaks favorably of Sanger's work on birth control, he could not gloss over Sanger's dark history as a eugenicist. Black writes:

> Sanger was an ardent, self-confessed eugenicist, and she would turn her otherwise noble birth control organizations into a tool for eugenics, which advocated mass sterilization of so-called defectives, mass incarceration of the unfit, and draconian immigration restrictions. Like other staunch eugenicists, Sanger vigorously opposed charitable efforts to uplift the downtrodden and deprived, and argued extensively that it was better that the cold and hungry be left without help, so that the eugenically superior could multiply without competition from "the unfit." She referred repeatedly to the lower classes and the unfit as "human waste" not worthy of assistance, and

proudly quoted the extreme eugenics view that human "weeds" should be exterminated.[4]

Dr. Robert Sussman, author of *The Myth of Race: The Troubling Persistence of an Unscientific Idea*, wrote the following about Sanger:

Margaret Sanger...advocated mass sterilization, incarceration of the unfit, and draconian immigration restrictions, and she included [Madison Grant's book] *Passing of the Great Race* on the eugenics reading list of her journal *Birth Control Review*. Madison Grant was the godfather of American scientific racism, and his book was called "the most influential tract of American scientific racism.[5]

Adolf Hitler quoted *Passing of the Great Race* often, yet Sanger continued to suggest this horrific book to her followers. It shouldn't surprise anyone that the author of this book is Madison Grant, the man who caged Ota Benga in the Bronx Zoo.

Author and speaker Ryan Bomberger writes:

To carry out her population control plans, her organization, American Birth Control League, that she founded in 1921, opened its facilities in predominantly black, immigrant, and poor areas of New York City (This would be the template for the majority of Planned Parenthood clinics). In 1939, with the help of wealthy American moguls (such as Clarence Gamble, of Procter & Gamble, and Mary Lasker) Sanger launched her racially motivated population control scheme that she called "The Negro Project," recruiting black preachers to sermonize her population control message. The aim of the Negro Project was to "severely reduce or eliminate" the reproduction of poorer blacks. As the American Birth Control League promoted this new program, Sanger and her fellow eugenicists pushed a program of African-American led indoctrination, birth control policies, and even sterilization throughout the United States.[6]

Today, Planned Parenthood is carrying out this agenda by its overwhelming presence in minority communities nationally. This thread is woven into many parts of our society. Remember, one of the other ways Sanger and other eugenicists sought to control the so-called "dysgenic" is through mass incarceration. Like most, I did not understand this eugenic connection between slavery, racism and abortion until a profound encounter I had while in prayer.

My understanding of God's heart over this issue started in June of 2001, when I had an experience of deep anguish during prayer that I'll never forget. I wept for more than two hours, as my heart broke over the marginalization of people and division in the nation regarding Native American issues, the slavery dilemma, and Jim Crow segregation. With an intensity I'd never known before, I wept over the pain and division between the races in America. Then I heard the Lord speak to me, "If I heard the whispered prayers of slaves underneath kettle pots, how much more do I hear the silent screams of babies being aborted in America?" It dawned on me how slavery and abortion are both inhumane. In the act of abortion, we kill that for which we once would have died and despise what others gave their lives to protect—the sanctity of human life.

Another unjust decree is upon the nation—the 1973 U.S. Supreme Court case *Roe v. Wade*. In similar form as *Dred Scott*, the Court said that babies in the womb have no human rights and no representation in court. Just like *Dred Scott*, that decision was passed 7 to 2. The dehumanizing similarities are eerie. In 1857, when people were outraged about the decision, Chief Justice Taney said that slaves fundamentally had no rights in a court of law. In 1973, in a 7 to 2 decision, when people were outraged over *Roe v. Wade*, Justice Blackmun basically said the fetus or unborn child has no rights in a court of law. Same dehumanizing arguments, different day. Both are unjust, and we have not learned the right lessons from history.

While many shout "Black Lives Matter," "All Lives Matter," and some "White Lives Matter," we must drill down deeper because God is saying, "Life Matters." He weeps over all the shedding of innocent blood. The God who wept over Ota Benga, Emmit Till, and Philando Castile (2016) is the same God who shed tears over the five police officers killed in Dallas (Brent Thompson, Patrick Zamarripa, Michael Krol, Michael Smith, and Lorne Ahrens), Heather Heyer killed in Charlottesville, (2017) and more than 60 million babies aborted in the womb (as of this writing). Will ending abortion fix all of our social ills? No, but can we honestly solve any problem in our communities while abortion still exists? When we dehumanize unborn people we cannot see and consider their lives optional, inevitably, it is easier to devalue some of the people we can see until their lives become marginal. We must keep pulling on the eugenic threads of racism and abortion until they are removed from the fabric of America.

Just as God addressed innocent bloodshed through slavery, He also wants us to address it through abortion today, which is the injustice that connected Matt and me years ago. On Martin Luther King, Jr. Day in 2005, Matt heard me speak for the first time about a new revival and justice movement, which included the baby in the womb, and ever since, we've been praying for a revival that will end abortion, before we even knew our shared family history. Our chance encounter was not a mistake, but one orchestrated by God, and such is the case with the child in the womb we've been called to protect. The other thread of this important dynamic is revealed in the dream Matt was given.

Matt speaking:

As you have seen, by going back a little further in history, we can trace the roots of abortion in the failed social engineering of the Eugenics Movement, which sought to remove from society those considered inferior and undesirable. Margaret Sanger was one of the most influential and resourceful people of the Eugenics Movement, and she founded Planned Parenthood, the largest abortion-provider in America, as a means to implement those racist ideals. Based on falsehoods, abortion-on-demand legitimized the wrongful mindset that children in the womb are optional. Agenda-driven people crafted careful vocabularies to dull the conscience of America. "It's not a baby. It's just a clump of tissue," became the crowning deception that allowed the nation to dehumanize and marginalize a new people group.

GOD'S DREAM IN THE WOMB

Remember in the last chapter when I talked about having that dream that radically changed my life, causing me to leave a career to become a missionary in Washington, DC? I must go into more detail of it now, so you can better understand the story that God has been weaving together.

That dream was actually about the ending of abortion. I want to point out the startling nature of the dream by saying that at that time in my life I didn't know anything about abortion. I'm sad to say that I didn't know anything about it because I didn't want to know anything about it. To me, abortion was one of those hot political topics I was content to leave to the dealings of others. It wasn't my focus because other things were more important to me. Maybe that mirrors your feelings, too.

As is often the case, all that changed with a dream from God. In my dream, I was in a large room filled with young people. On one wall of the room was an enormous chalkboard covered with facts and figures about abortion, and all of the young people were holding chalkboard erasers in their hands. To my surprise, instead of trying to erase what was on the board, they all began to pray loudly at the same time. Each time one of them would say a prayer, he or she would step up to the chalkboard and smack their eraser against it. The impact of the eraser would then create a cloud of white dust. In my dream, the volume got louder and louder as the young people continued to pray all night long. Sometime in the middle of the night—it seemed to be around 3:00 a.m.—I looked over and saw a man, and I knew his name was Lou Engle. I approached him and asked, "How do you function the next day when you do this all night?" He responded,

"I DON'T KNOW!" Then he turned and hit the chalkboard even harder. At the end of the night I saw out a window that the sun was rising, and I looked back at the chalkboard. What was written on the board had not been erased. Instead, it had been made completely white by all the impacts of the erasers.

It is no exaggeration to say that I have never been quite the same since having that dream. As I discussed in the previous chapter, there was the remarkable part about meeting Lou Engle before I knew him, and it was provocative that what I had seen in the dream so closely mirrored what God was leading him to do. It was all quite effective in getting me to move my family to Washington, D.C. However, something bigger was being communicated through it all. Allow me to break down the dream a bit as I have come to understand it. I believe the details reveal the heart of God in all this.

In the dream, God showed me His desire for an entire generation to contend in prayer for the ending of abortion. The task sounds impossible to some, but I have learned through experience that God answers prayer. He initiates things as a way for us to partner with him. Jesus taught us to pray, "Your kingdom come, your will be done, on earth as it is in heaven" (Matthew 6:10). God will make His will known, and then we get to agree with Him and pray that will into being. Arthur Wallis said it like this, "If you would do the best with your life, find out what God is doing in your generation and throw yourself wholly into it."[7] The question is what all does God want to do in this generation?

In my dream, God introduced me to His dream. The subject of abortion wasn't something that bubbled up from my subconscious or the activities of the day. I didn't care about it at all, but just because it wasn't important to me didn't mean it wasn't extremely important to God. The baby in the womb is nothing less than the manifest dream of God. Think about it this way: At some point, God dreamed a dream. He wrapped flesh and bone around it, and you're the embodiment of that dream. The situations and circumstances that preceded you, no matter how tragic, were merely the unique conditions of your arrival. Scripture explains:

> And he made from one man every nation of mankind to live on all the face of the earth, having determined allotted periods and the boundaries of their dwelling place, that they should seek God, and perhaps feel their way toward him and find him. Yet he is actually not far from each one of us, for "In him we live and move and have our being"; as even some of your own poets have said, "For we are indeed his offspring." (Acts 17:26-28)

God determined when and where we would live, the family we would be born into, the neighborhood we would grow up in, and the conditions of our lives that would lead us to search for Him. God was not surprised when any of us got here. No divine sneeze produced anyone's unexpected existence and left Him wondering what to do. No one is an accident.

Modern science has destroyed the decades-old argument that pregnancy is just a clump of tissue. King David's words echo with perfect application today, "For you formed my inward parts; you knitted me together in my mother's womb. I praise you, for I am fearfully and wonderfully made. Wonderful are your works; my soul knows it very well." (Psalm 139:13-14)

In my dream, the young people were holding erasers, but they weren't erasing what was on the chalkboard. That's because the court case *Roe v. Wade* is responsible for the loss of more than 60 million dreams of God (at the writing of this book). We must come to grips with the fact that the baby in the womb is a real human being, and we cannot trivialize its death. Incarnate Jesus in Mary's womb was no less human than baby Jesus in the manger, the 12-year-old in the temple, or the 33-year-old hanging on the cross. The Divine put on humanity at the moment of conception, and the angel Gabriel announced that glorious reality to Mary.

Another curious part of the dream is the dust clouds created by each eraser. They represented the impact made by each prayer that is in agreement with God's heart for this travesty to end. I believe that is especially important given Lou's odd response of, "I don't know," when I asked him how the group functions. Typically, people want to work things out and strategize plans before they ever get started. Lou's answer in the dream highlights the urgency of the moment and the need for immediate prayer even before we have the details figured out. The cumulative effect of all the prayers is then evident. The chalkboard is a lesson to us that what has happened cannot be erased. It can, however, be made white (see Isa. 1:18).

In the months following the dream, when I was asking God to speak to me about whether I should go to Washington, DC, I received a beautiful confirmation when my oldest daughter had a strong encounter of her own with the Lord that influenced my decision. At the time, Taylor was 10 and already loved to read. She would often read to her younger brothers. One evening she walked into the kitchen where I was standing with a serious look on her face and said, "Daddy, I think I found something important." What an odd thing for such a young person to say. "What do you mean?" I asked. "I was reading this book to my brothers, and I think it means something." She then showed me an old beloved children's book written by Dr. Seuss. The book was *Horton Hears a Who*, and she opened it to show me the key line repeated throughout the story: "A person's a person, no matter how small."[8] I knew God was confirming to me that I was to go to DC in obedience to the dream, but I could then see that He was also inviting me to a multi-generational call.

I believe God showed me in my dream His heart for the ending of abortion. What we all must wrestle with is the fact that it was this dream that led me to DC where I met Will. The issues of racism and abortion are like tragic scarlet threads woven together through our nation's history. That revelation was soon to take on profound meaning.

UNCONDITIONAL SURRENDER

The Word of God should always be the foundation for ministry, not subjective dreams. However, in scripture we see that God strategically used dreams to bring encouragement, warning, and unique insight. A dream had given me information for how to respond to God and to move to Washington, DC to be a part of the Justice House of Prayer. In the early days of JHOP, as we call it, we received another dream from the Lord that gave us important language and urgency for our mandate to pray for the ending of abortion.

In this dream, a young leader and the JHOP company were moving through a large building filled with courtrooms, going from one courtroom to another. They came to a long hallway that led to a large courtroom called the "Appomattox Room." In it, preparations were being made to hear the *Roe v. Wade* case.

This dream about the Appomattox Room has always been a sobering word from the Lord to us. It came during a time of intensified fasting and prayer for a specific case that was put before the U.S. Supreme Court to re-hear *Roe v. Wade* in 2005— one they refused to hear at that time. The dream is a window into God's desire to see that tragic decision overturned in our courts. It highlights both the opportunity and the warning of the Lord for our time. It is an invitation to partner with God to see His great purpose manifested in the earth, but it is also a stark reminder of God's desire to make wrong things right.

Thomas Jefferson once commented about slavery in Virginia:

And can the liberties of a nation be thought secure when we have removed their only firm basis, a conviction in the minds of the people that these liberties are of the gift of God? That they are not to be violated but with his wrath? Indeed I tremble for my country when I reflect that God is just: that his justice cannot sleep for ever: that considering numbers, nature and natural means only, a revolution of the wheel of fortune, an exchange of situation is among possible events: that it may become probable by supernatural interference![9]

Jefferson's words ought to be terrifying to us. This quote is carved in the stone of the Jefferson Memorial in Washington, DC. These words echo across the Potomac Tidal Basin in the Lincoln Memorial, too, where similar words of warning are etched, taken from Abraham Lincoln's Second Inaugural Address. Consider that Lincoln lived in the tragic reality that Jefferson imagined. How many tourists every year look up at those engraved words and take no thought of what those lingering truths might mean for the nation today?

For many years, that dream about the courtrooms has provided us with vivid language for prayer and intercession: "Mercy, O God! We don't want to be driven back to another Appomattox." What in the world does that prayer mean? Remember from the previous chapters how significant Appomattox Court House became to the story. A brief American history lesson is probably needed at this point.

In April 1865, General Robert E. Lee was in retreat across Virginia with his Confederate army, and he made it as far as Appomattox Court House. Overcome by the Union army, it was there he signed papers of unconditional surrender to General Ulysses Grant on April 9. That event marked the end of the American Civil War. It also represented the largest death toll of any war in American history. New estimates indicate that approximately 750,000 people lost their lives in that four-year conflict.[10]

Appomattox is a bloody reminder for this nation, and the fact that God drew our attention to it in the dream is both shocking and revealing. The dream connected the injustice of our nation's tragic past with those happening today right in front of us. God gave us the understanding of the dream, saying to us, "Either you deal with *Roe v. Wade* in your courts, or I will deal with it in mine." This revelation has been key for me through many years of prayer. In response to it, God has given me a national prayer mobilization strategy called Bound4LIFE that is contending for the ending of abortion with an ongoing special focus on the courts, and Will Ford was part of the original board of directors. We have seen the prayers of this organization make tremendous impact on lawmakers and court cases as well as bring healing to individuals in pain.

UNITING AS ONE VOICE

Will speaking:

Part of the pain Matt mentions here is my own. January 17, 2005, when I spoke in the conference where Matt and I met, I also shared a painful memory. For the first time, I shared that I paid for the abortion of a child I fathered in college. After sharing my testimony and journey of healing, we called men forward for prayer. We then knelt before women who once had abortions, and we asked for their forgiveness for not wanting to be the father of their children, abandoning them in their time of need, and manipulating them into doing something they would regret for the rest of their lives. Many men and women, young and old, were deeply moved and healed.

Cathy Harris was profoundly impacted by the ministry time that night. Once the conference was over, she went back home and felt the leading of the Lord to start prayer meetings with her new friend, Liz Robertson. As they began to build their friendship and share their passion for praying for revival and the ending of abortion, they realized they both were at the same conference in DC where I had spoken. Their prayer meeting eventually became one of Matt's Bound4LIFE chapters in Atlanta. Discovering there were 12 abortion centers in the city, they chose one as their focus.

Their prayer meeting at the clinic went from once-a-month to twice-a-month. It started out with two people and grew into as many as 20 to 40 people praying together. I received an email they sent out, and unbeknownst to them, of the 12 abortion centers they could have chosen, they selected the clinic where I had paid for the abortion of my child more than 30 years ago. I had never shared the state, city, or location of that facility publicly. After I prayed for Cathy's healing in DC, the Dream King sent her to the very place where I had paid for the abortion I so regretted.

During Mother's Day weekend of 2007, Matt and I traveled to pray with Cathy, Liz, and the rest of the Bound4LIFE team at that abortion center. That day, we saw five women change their minds about aborting their children, and they got the assistance they needed. Later that year, one of their team members had a dream in which she was told, "If you hold this prayer meeting for 40 days straight, this abortion center will shut down." These young people took this dream as a prayer assignment from God and prayed in front of the clinic for 40 days straight. At the end of 40 days, the security guard, who began to befriend the group, said, "Well, what you all are doing must be paying off, because this clinic is going to shut down at the end of November." They were ecstatic. Sure enough, a note posted saying the clinic was closed, and no abortions have taken place at that location since; the building remains empty. As God would have it, that abortion center's closing occurred on November 30th, which is my birthday.

As of this writing, the abortionist is in prison, exposed for Medicaid fraud, and all of the abortion centers he owned no longer exist. As part of God's dream, I believe this all happened on my birthday as a sign that every person conceived deserves to have a birthday, and no one is a mistake. Transformed hearts produce transformed laws, which is why we are contending for another Great Awakening. In the next chapter, we learn the hidden history of the Christian slaves God used to transform America.

Chapter 5

SECRET SANCTUARIES

Will speaking:

By now, you may be wondering how I started in ministry, traveling with the kettle around the country, before meeting Matt. Just like our chance encounter, a providential series of divine appointments not only launched me into ministry but also led me to uncover the spiritual life of Christian slaves in America. In this chapter I want to connect to an essential part of our nation's fabric, which has kept our country together: The hidden spiritual legacy of worship and prayer of Christian African American slaves. First, let's start with how I began my ministry of prayer in 2001, which eventually led to meeting Matt in 2005.

Before this profound connection to my family heritage and the kettle, I was an average Christian leader, a husband, a father, a businessman, and a spiritual mentor to youth. I had served as a church lay minister for about 15 years. I'd been a student of revival and had prayed for it for many years. In August 2000, as my hunger for revival began to grow intensely, I felt the Lord calling me into 40 days of fasting and prayer. On the first day of the fast, someone spray-painted my neighbor's car. No one had committed this sort of random vandalism in my neighborhood before, so I decided to begin walking, not for exercise, but for prayer, doing what we like to call "prayer walking."

At first, my prayer walks were about asking God for protection. I'd take my Bible and declare Scripture promises over my neighborhood, my city of Euless, Texas, and the nation. During this time, I also studied about the First and Second Great Awakenings, as well as the Azusa Street revival in America, and I began crying out for another awakening in our day. At the time, I had no idea this was preparing me for a national conference and tour about prayer and revival in America. God Himself did this by connecting me to my family's history of prayer at a conference in Colorado Springs.

A CONNECTION AND AN OFFER

A short time after the fast, in March 2001, I chose to go to a conference in Colorado Springs, Colorado, where I heard a message by a man named Dutch Sheets that marked me for life concerning agreement in prayer and the synergy created by joining with the prayers of our forefathers. This phrase struck me: "Not only can we agree in prayer with the person next to us, but we can also agree in prayer with generations behind us." I began to see that when we understand what previous generations prayed for and God's purposes, we can move the spiritual momentum forward exponentially. Jesus' words, "Greater works than these are you going to do, because I am going to the Father" (John 14: 12) took on a deeper meaning for me.

After Dutch spoke, I approached him and related to him the history of my family's black kettle. Overwhelmed and awe-struck, to my surprise, he asked that I share it with the others at the conference. On the last day of the gathering, he said that he felt we should stay in touch with each other. During my time at the conference, I was unexpectedly called out of the audience, because of my name being William, to participate in prayer for a potential conference in Williamsburg, Virginia. By that time, Dutch was beginning to feel that I should play a direct part in that conference.

Afterwards, I began to sense this was more than a moment of shared hype or emotionalism, and God was really up to something. After prayer, research, and the leading of the Holy Spirit, I began to receive a series of coincidences that caught my attention, which could only be brought to my awareness by the providential hand of the Dream King Himself. Essentially, I learned that the street signs in my neighborhood, had become providential guide-posts. It's true: when we pray, coincidences happen, orchestrated by the Dream King.

I later received an email from Dutch saying that he felt we were to go not only to Williamsburg, but also throughout all of New England and the Northeast to pray for revival. Neither of us had ever mentioned New England in our conversations before, but I remembered studying the New England revivals while prayer-walking my neighborhood during my 40-day fast. Had God been preparing me for this in a specific way? I agreed that I was open to going, but I still needed more confirmation. I began asking, "God, is this really you?"

My remaining doubts were erased a few weeks later when Dutch sent me a list of the cities for the prayer tour. In a very profound way, I saw that God indeed had prepared me for this prayer journey. I realized that for two years I had been prayer walking streets named after the very cities and regions of our projected tour.

For instance, I noticed that Jamestown, one of the original American settlements, was one of our destinations—Jamestown Court was the name of the street across from me. We were to go to Princeton University—Princeton Street was two blocks behind me. New Haven, Connecticut, was on the list—New Haven Court was one block down from my house. Also on tour was Plymouth, Massachusetts—Plymouth Court was across from New Haven Court in my neighborhood. Gettysburg, Pennsylvania—Gettysburg Street was around the corner from me. Dartmouth University—Dartmouth Court was four blocks down from my house. Hanover, New Hampshire—Hanover Street is right next to Princeton Street.

On it went. We were to visit Williamsburg, Annapolis, and Washington, D.C. All of these cities are in the Chesapeake Bay area, and my house was on Chesapeake Street. Potomac, Warwick, Middlebury, Trenton, Rochester, New Bedford, Nantucket, and Saratoga were on Dutch's list—and they, too, were all streets in my neighborhood. Basically, I had been prayer walking cities of New England and America's original settlements—and doing it while in Texas. When God gets this serious about the details, it's a sign that He is inviting us to partner with Him. For me, the invitation was to enter into the unfinished business of praying for the next generation, by continuing the work of prayer from the previous generation in my family.

GOD'S GREAT PLAN

Suddenly, this all became more symbolic and meaningful. Why would God have all this happen through a white man named Dutch and an African American man named William III? I believe that God used us as a symbolic picture of what He wanted to do in the nation. The Dutch were the first people to bring slaves ships to America in 1619, and William III was one of the first kings to send slave ships here. God brought us together and is using our relationship to demonstrate that He wants to bring a new level of healing to America and reverse the effects of yesterday's pain. Dutch once said to me, "Wouldn't it be just like God, in His irony and justice, to use the age-old prayers of a slave generation—along with their cooking, washing, and prayer bowl—as a part of bringing revival and spiritual freedom to a generation of Americans today?" We were both speechless.

On our journey, called The Kettle Tour, we traveled the country for about a month, praying for revival and healing of the races in America throughout New England and the North Eastern portion of the nation. And in every place we went, we carried the kettle from my family, using it as a reminder of the prayer bowls in heaven. We also used it as a memorial for those who had gone before us. The Kettle Tour of 2001 launched me into national ministry, and I've been traveling and speaking on prayer, unity, and revival ever since. Dutch became a mentor to me, and together we co-wrote my first book, *History Makers*.

As we mentioned before, my ancestor's kettle was used by the Lord as a reminder of the prayer bowls in heaven. God gave us a specific verse of Scripture as a confirmation, "The cooking pots in the Lord's house will be like the bowls before the altar"

(Zechariah 14:20). This old kettle in my family caught the muffled prayers of slaves in the same way that bowls in Heaven catch the incense of our prayers (Revalation 5:8). This story of my family kettle led me to research many American slave narratives to see if I could find similarities in other African American families. The first question I had was, "Why was it necessary for slaves to have secret prayer meetings and secret church services?"

Matt speaking:

First, we must understand how the white settlers sought to control the rapidly growing slave population. The Virginia colony led the way in the new world with its transition from indentured servitude to slavery. Beginning in 1705, legal codes were put in place that seemed to seal the fate of African Americans forever.

> All servants imported and brought into the Country… who were not Christians in their native Country…shall be accounted and be slaves. All Negro, mulatto and Indian slaves within this dominion…shall be held to be real estate. If any slave resist his master…correcting such slave, and shall happen to be killed in such correction… the master shall be free of all punishment…as if such accident never happened.[1]

The systematic break down of human rights paved the way for increasingly strict handling of slaves' mobility and opportunity to learn:

That all meetings or assemblages of slaves, or free negroes or mulattoes mixing and associating with such slaves at any meeting-house or houses, etc., in the night; or at any school or schools for teaching them reading or writing, either in the day or night, under whatsoever pretext, shall be deemed and considered an unlawful assembly; and any justice of a county, etc., wherein such assemblage shall be, either from his own knowledge or the information of others, of such unlawful assemblage, etc., may issue his warrant, directed to any sworn officer or officers, authorizing him or them to enter the house or houses where such unlawful assemblages, etc., may be, for the purpose of apprehending or dispersing such slaves, and to inflict corporal punishment on the offender or offenders, at the discretion of any justice of the peace, not exceeding twenty lashes.[2]

These types of restrictions and punishments became common throughout the Southern states. There were exceptions made for religious purposes, but even those were to be taken away in time.

Will speaking:

In addition to what Matt has mentioned, I learned that slaves were previously allowed to have religious meetings of their own, but after the thwarted revolts and insurrection attempts of some slaves, they were forbidden to even meet to worship. Also, slave masters didn't want slaves to gain a desire for freedom, which is another reason they were forbidden to pray. Often they were flogged if they were found singing or praying at home. Some slave masters justified their mistreatment of the slaves, claiming slaves had no souls and therefore could not receive the gift of eternal life. Nevertheless, some slaves who had become Christians, because of their love for Christ, risked their lives to worship and pray in their own meetings.

Moses Grandy told in his slave narrative what happened to his brother-in-law, who was brutally beaten and his back "pickled" for praying and preaching in the woods. Pickling, as Grandy described in his story, was when, after whipping, once the back was ripped open, pork or beef brine was intentionally poured into the open wounds to create more pain. He wrote:

> They may go to the places of worship used by the whites; but they like their meetings better. My wife's brother Isaac was a colored preacher. A number of slaves went privately into the woods to hold meetings; when they were found out, they were flogged, and each was forced to tell who else was there.

> Three were shot, two of whom were killed and the other was badly wounded. For preaching to them, Isaac was flogged, and his back pickled; when it was nearly well, he was flogged and pickled again, and so on for some months; then his back was suffered to get well, and he was sold. A little while before this, his wife was sold away with an infant at her breast; and out of six children, four had been sold away one by one at a time. On the way with his buyers he dropped down dead; his heart was broke."[3]

This harrowing account reveals not only the cruelty of slavery, but also the willingness of devout Christian slaves to seek their Savior in prayer; regardless of the consequences, they prayed anyway. Like the stories passed down in my family, many Christian slave narratives show how their ancestors yearned to hold underground gatherings because they wanted to pray for freedom and desired more of God.

This discovery led me to a study of slave narratives from across the country. I learned that, like my ancestors, a remnant of Christian slaves on plantations also used kettles and other containers to conceal their prayer meetings. Edd Roby from Mississippi recalls:

> Our white Marsa didn't 'low his slaves to read an' 'rite. Went to de white folks church an' den wouldn't low 'em to pray. Would whip 'em when day catched [slaves] prayin' at home or anywhere else. Dey told me 'bout one old woman on de place dat prayed a heep but she allus put her head down in de pot when she went to pray so as de white folks couldn't hear her.[4]

MORE CAST IRON KETTLES

According to Albert J. Raboteau, professor of religion at Princeton University, slaves often used kettles to conceal their prayer meetings:

> The most common device for preserving secrecy was an iron pot usually placed in the middle of the cabin floor or at the doorstep, then slightly propped up to hold the

sound of the praying and singing from escaping. A variation was to pray or sing softly "with heads together around" the "kettle to deaden the sound."[5]

I found hundreds of written examples from Christian slaves across the country who used wash pots, barrels, and kettles to muffle their voices as they prayed. According to historians I've spoken with, as slaves were sold across the country, this method of concealing their prayers was carried along with them, which spread this type of prayer meeting across the country. Many accounts mentioned how a secret code song was used to alert everyone of the prayer meetings at night. The song was called "Steal Away With Jesus." Former slave Wash Wilson recalls:

When de [slaves] go round singin' 'Steal Away to Jesus,' dat mean dere gwine be a 'ligious meetin' dat night. De masters…didn't like dem 'ligious meetin's so us natcherly slips off at night, down in de bottoms or somewhere. Sometimes us sing and pray all night.[6]

Laura Thornton, a former slave from Arkansas, said:

Ole boss wold tie em tuh a tree and whoop em if dey caught us even praying. We had er big black washpot an de way we prayed we'd go out an put our mouths to der groun and pray low and de sound wud go up under de pot an ole boss couldn't hear us.[7]

Former slave Alex Woods of North Carolina recalled:

Dey would not allow us to have prayer meetings in our houses, but we would gather late in de night and turn pots upside down inside de door to kill de sound and sing and pray for freedom. No one could hear unless dey eaves-drapped.[8]

Because of the danger, the slaves who prayed under pots appointed lookouts to alert them if the master or his overseers were coming. As the lookouts watched, others prayed, using barrels, iron wash pots, and cooking kettles to muffle their voices. In her narrative, Kitty Hill recounted:

Dey turned pots down ter kill de noise an' held meetings at night. Dey had [slaves] ter watch an' give de alarm if dey saw de [overseers]. Dey always looked out for [patrollers].[9]

I found more than 300 descriptions of slaves having secret prayer meetings, and more than half used pots, barrels, and other means to muffle their voices to pray for freedom. Many accounts also include digging holes in the ground to pray, sometimes in conjunction with these vessels. Once in the hole, they put the pot or barrel on top to cover them as they prayed, preventing their prayers from being heard.

Ex-slave Ellen Butler recalls:

Dey hab big holes out in de fiel's dey git down in and pray. Dey done dat way 'cause de w'ite folks didn' want 'em to pray. Dey uster pray for freedom.[10]

Instead of being used ritually, these methods were used practically as an acoustic means to conceal their prayer times for fear of being caught and punished. When asked why they used this way to conceal their voices, one former slave replied, "I don't know where they learned to do that. I kinda think the Lord put them things in their minds to do for themselves, just like he helps us Christians in other ways. Don't you think so?"[11] Hebrews 11:38 says these were people of whom the world was not worthy, who dwelt in "holes in the ground," and under cooking pots—I add—praying for you and for me.

HOLY HUSH TABERNACLES

In his slave narrative, Peter Randolph revealed how slaves also concealed prayer meetings by building temporary tabernacles, called "brush harbors" or "hush harbors." In the dark of night, those first to the selected spot bent the boughs of trees as they walked along in the direction of the prayer meeting. Those following behind felt which direction these branches were bent, which guided them to the prayer meeting. After arriving in the desired location, they soaked quilts with water, which were used to build four walls around them. This created a tabernacle. The wet blankets helped to deaden the sound as they prayed.[12]

Interestingly, this manner of prayer is reminiscent of Israel's escape from Egyptian slavery, as they built tents to tabernacle with God in the wilderness. Still today, Jews have an observance called the "Feast of Tabernacles," commemorating when God led them out of slavery: "Speak unto the children of Israel, saying, 'The fifteenth day of this seventh month shall be the feast of tabernacles for seven days unto the LORD.'" (Leviticus 23:34 KJV)

The reason for this celebration is stated later in the passage: "...so that your generations may know that I had the sons of Israel live in booths (tabernacles) when I brought them out from the land of Egypt. I am the LORD your God" (Leviticus 23:42-43 KJV). The Hebrew word *succoth* means booth, dwelling, or tabernacle. The point here is that much like the slaves who prayed under kettle pots to muffle their voices, those praying in Hush Harbor tabernacles with wet blankets were merely using this method as an acoustic means to absorb the sound of their prayers. The Israelites had no home of their own as they were delivered out of slavery. Just as the Israelite slaves were led to live and meet with God in temporary cloth tents in the wilderness, American slaves found God in similar water-soaked tabernacles in the woods. Scripture says that God determines the boundaries of our dwellings, so that people would, "perhaps feel their way toward him and find him (Acts 17:26-27 NLT). The slaves who slipped off, feeling their way through the dark, did just that.

Mr. Randolph gives an account of the prayer meetings he attended:

The male members then select a certain space, in separate groups, for the division of the meeting. Preaching... by the brethren, then praying and singing all around, until they generally feel quite happy. The speaker usually commences by calling himself unworthy, and talks very slowly, until feeling the spirit, he grows excited, and in a short time, there fall to the ground twenty or thirty men and women under its influence...[13]

James Washington, in his book *Conversations With God*, chronicles the prayers of former slaves. In the following excerpt, an anonymous slave intercedes, starting by referencing Psalm 137:1-4. He or she then makes entreaty for the Civil War and freedom and ends by praying for ensuing generations:

Masser Jesus, like de people ob de ole time, de Jews, we weep by the side ob de ribber, wid de srings ob de harp all broken. But we sing ob de broken heart, as dem people could not do so. Hear us King, in our present state of sorrows…Help us for our own good, and de good ob God's blessed Union people, dat want all people free, whatsomebedder de color…Master Jesus, you know de deep tribulation ob our hearts, dat our children dying in de camp, and as we tote dem from one place to tudder, and bury dem in de cold ground, Jesus, to go in spirit, to de God of de people whare de soul hab no spot nor color. Great King ob Kings, and Doctor ob Doctors, and God ob Battles, help us to be well. Help us to be able to fight wid de Union sogers de battle for de Union—help us to fight for liberty—fight for de country—fight for our homes, and our own free children, and our children's children.[14]

THE POWER OF PRAYER

In our book *History Makers*, Dutch Sheets and I write:

Prayers offered in secret, wet-blanket tabernacles and muffled under cast-iron kettles filled golden prayer bowls in Heaven. It's exciting to think that our prayers are stored in the same place. Note that in Revelation 5:8, "bowls" is plural. We don't know how many bowls hold our prayers, but it's very likely that each of us has his or her bowl in Heaven. I don't know if they are literal or symbolic, and it doesn't matter. The principle is still the same—God stores our prayers for use at the proper time. It is awesome to think our prayers go up to Heaven as incense and are collected inside bowls before God's altar. At the right time, God turns these bowls over and pours out a powerful release in answer to prayers:

Revelation 8 gives a powerful glimpse of what is happening in the heavenly realm:

And another angel came and stood over the altar, having a golden censer; and there was given unto him much incense, that he should add it unto the prayers of all the saints upon the golden altar which was before the throne. And the smoke of the incense, with the prayers of the saints, went up before God out of the angel's hand. And the angel taketh the censer, and he filled it with the fire of the altar, and cast it upon the earth: and there followed thunders, and voices, and lightning, and an earthquake (Revelation 8:3-5, ASV).

It is amazing to ponder that when the fire fell on Sinai and the fire fell at Pentecost, these things happened as a result of someone's prayers on earth. According to this passage, that same fire is mixed with the bowl of our prayers in heaven. Then, when God determines the time is right, He hurls these bowls upon the earth, and in the heavenlies, lightening flashes and thunder are released, and earthquakes are manifested as a result of our prayers. There is not one wasted prayer in heaven. The power released in the spiritual realm provides the results manifested in the natural realm.

TIP THE BOWLS!

Quiet but fervent prayers for freedom offered underneath kettles joined with the prayers and sermons of the Great Awakenings, were answered. One day God tipped over their prayer bowls in Heaven and changed society.

Speaking in Senegal, one of the largest slave trading ports in Africa and the world during slavery, President George W. Bush, in a powerful speech on the subject of American slavery, said:

In America, enslaved Africans learned the story of the exodus from Egypt and set their own hearts on a promised land of freedom. Enslaved Africans discovered a suffering Savior and found he was more like themselves than their masters. Enslaved Africans heard the ringing promises of the Declaration of Independence and asked the self-evident question, "Then why not me?" That deliverance was demanded by escaped slaves named Frederick Douglass and Sojourner Truth...Booker T. Washington...and ministers of the gospel named Leon Sullivan and Martin Luther King, Jr....We can discern eternal standards in the deeds of William Wilberforce and John Quincy Adams and Harriet Beecher Stowe and Abraham Lincoln. These men and women, black and white, burned with a zeal for freedom, and they left behind a different and better nation. Their moral vision caused Americans to examine our hearts, to correct our Constitution, and to teach our children the dignity and equality of every person of every race. By a plan known only to Providence, the stolen sons and daughters of Africa helped to awaken the conscience of America. The very people traded into slavery helped to set America free.[15]

These eloquent words of President Bush capture the irony of God using those enslaved in America to set the nation morally free. Our prayer is for another epic spiritual awakening that breaks every chain in America. Think of it: Wouldn't it be like God, in His justice and irony, to remember the prayers of a slave generation, mix them with ours and free a nation once again through another powerful Great Awakening? Oh God, we pray again, tip the bowls!

Chapter 6

WHAT STORYLINE DO YOU WANT TO BE A PART OF?

Matt speaking:

We all have questionable things in our backgrounds. I have done bad stuff. Will has made regrettable choices in his past. All of our families have skeletons stuffed in their proverbial closets—things we'd just like to forget. For many people, though, there are destructive themes that have become dominating storylines, often spanning multiple generations. Breaking out of these patterns can seem impossible. Perhaps you are stuck in a never-ending cycle of bad decisions, but you already know that your parents wrestled with the same things. You feel like the recipient of a horrible curse set in motion long ago.

We have to grapple with the questions of what defines us. What is the driving storyline of your life? America is in a storyline crisis right now, and many would-be storytellers are grasping for control of the narrative. One element that stands out as a bloody stain in the collective history of America is the issue of slavery. It still casts a long shadow stretching through hundreds of years and affecting lives today.

I can't think of anything more despicable than subjugating another human being and presuming to own that person as property. As the intricate story emerged of how Will's family and mine had been woven together, imagine how I felt when I discovered that my part of the story was connected to that of the slave owner. The story, however, was about to make an unexpected turn yet again. I was about to uncover another piece of the puzzle that would have redemptive power and release unknown blessing.

NATIONAL SHAME

Today when we look back at our national history of slavery, it's hard to imagine how we could have ever done such a thing. While slavery could be found almost everywhere in the world up through the nineteenth century, John Wesley, the great English Methodist preacher, called America's version of slavery "the vilest that ever saw the sun."[1] Try as we might, we can't hide this bloodstain in our national fabric.

When the topic of slavery enters the picture, it has a profound effect on people. The PBS documentary series *Finding Your Roots* has uncovered many family histories of slave ownership in the backgrounds of top celebrities. Actor Ben Affleck had to publicly apologize after it was leaked that he pressured the show's producers to edit out his relationship to slave owners.[2] He claimed that the shame from it was just too much for him. It's interesting that his efforts to cover up the sins of the past were unsuccessful. What an important lesson for us all to learn.

Martin Luther King, Jr. famously highlighted in his *I Have A Dream* speech in 1963 that black people were still languishing in the corners of American society a century after the Emancipation Proclamation. As the nation now hovers at the 50-year anniversary of his assassination, we are all still wrestling with questions of systemic racism. Some things have changed, and yet some things have remained the same. The Civil Rights movement exposed the shame of racial injustice and provoked some change. The national conscience was confronted, yet old patterns persist another half century later.

Jesus dealt with a similar delusional condition in his generation. He addressed the leaders of his day saying:

Woe to you, scribes and Pharisees, hypocrites! For you build the tombs of the prophets and decorate the monuments of the righteous, saying, "If we had lived in the days of our fathers, we would not have taken part with them in shedding the blood of the prophets." Thus you witness against yourselves that you are sons of those who murdered the prophets. Fill up, then, the measure of your fathers. (Matthew 23:29-32)

The deceitfulness of sin is apparent in this. As people carelessly float down a river of sin in their own day, they daydream that they would have swum against the current in former days. Here, they claim that if they had the opportunities of the past to honor the prophets, they would never have killed them, yet, as Matthew Henry points out, they were plotting to murder *The* Prophet at that very moment.[3]

The opportunities of the present moment to alter a storyline filled with curses must not be wasted. The warning issued here was ominous as Jesus spoke of an accumulated heaping up of historical consequences that would be brought upon the heads of one generation. For them it was the devastation of 70 A.D. For our American ancestors, it was the devastation of the Civil War. What clouds are gathering over our heads even now if we fail to swim against the current of sin?

For years I had admired Will's telling of the kettle story. My faith and imagination were ignited every time I heard of the slaves who prayed in secret for abolition. It never got old for me to hear about their rich heritage of faithful perseverance. However, the dark side of their oppression was abstract to me because it seemed so far removed. It was easy for me to be emotionally disconnected from "those people." Yet for many African Americans, images of plantations and recollections about the cruelty of overseers serve as powerful reminders of the pain of the past that frames their lives and experiences today. My point of view in all this dramatically changed when it was revealed that it was actually my family who owned Will's family. Suddenly, I had to process the reality of that history in a very personal way. I could feel the shame associated with it because now it had a face—one that I knew and loved. I found myself in a moment of confrontation with the wrongs of the past, and a response was being demanded from me.

COMFORTING GOD

Will speaking:

I have experienced what it feels like to know God's heart when it is broken over a situation. During the Kettle Tour in 2001, I had an experience of deep travail in prayer that I'll never forget. I wept for more than two hours as my heart was broken over division and the marginalization of people in the nation—from the first settlers with the Native Americans to the enslavement of Africans leading to Jim Crow segregation. While praying and seeking to find out what was happening to me, I was reminded of the prayer walks God led me to do in my neighborhood. I heard the Lord say to me, "William, you walked me through your neighborhood; now I'm walking you through my neighborhood. I'm sharing with you my heart for America."

When God shares his concerns with us, our prayers on behalf of others not only lead to comfort for the victimized, but they also comfort God's heart. Could He really need comfort? Is justice really that important to God? Isaiah 59 gives us the answer.

Justice is turned back, and righteousness stands far away; for truth has stumbled in the public squares, and uprightness cannot enter. Truth is lacking, and he who departs from evil makes himself a prey. The Lord saw it, and it displeased him that there was no justice. He saw that there was no man, and wondered that there was no one to intercede; then his own arm brought him salvation, and his righteousness upheld him. (Isaiah 59:14-16)

Take note of two important words in these verses: "displeased" and "wondered." Understanding of these words reveals God's heart over injustice. The Hebrew word for displeased comes from the root meaning "to be broken up."[4] The Hebrew word for wondered means "to be desolate, be appalled, stun, stupefy."[5] Think of it this way: When God sees injustice, His heart shatters or is broken. He then seeks someone on Earth who shares His heart about this burden. When our hearts ache over the injustice like His, our prayers bring relief and comfort to His heart. When He can't find anyone who is concerned about injustice, He is astonished, stunned, and devastated.

HEALING THE PAST

Matt speaking:

I don't think it does anyone justice to deny the reality of these past wrongs. The more pressing question is, "Are those the storylines that will dominate our future?" So much work has been done in recent years in the area of racial reconciliation. I have personally had the privilege of participating in many moments of healing when leaders have felt led to deal with the sins of the past by repenting on behalf of our forbearers. These things are not to be ignored, as some would have it when they flippantly say, "It's time just to move on." Nor are they things to be used to perpetually shame others into an unending pattern of penance, as some would equally have it.

Washing the feet of another is a powerful demonstration of a contrite heart and an expression of love. It's a humbling picture provided to us by Jesus himself when he knelt down to wash the feet of his disciples. Will and I have actually washed each other's feet in the kettle used by his ancestors for prayer. In fact, many feet have been washed in that kettle, including the children of Martin Luther King, Jr. We actually did that on the historic steps of the Lincoln Memorial in 2016, right where their father gave the *I Have a Dream* speech.

King once said, "It may be true that the law cannot make a man love me, but it can keep him from lynching me, and I think that's pretty important."[6] If the previous generation only succeeded in regulating behavior, it is up to this generation to complete the work—the greater work—of changing the heart.

Those who genuinely want to heal the nation have tapped into an alternate ending to the story. The spirit of hate and rage would have white and black destroy each other in an uninterrupted climax of human tragedy, but God is releasing his great mercy strategy right now that can bring healing to history's hemorrhaging wounds. The work of Christians engaged in racial reconciliation and healing plays an important part in the story because it doesn't just attempt to put a Band-Aid on current issues. Instead, it acknowledges the injustice of the past, and through profound acts of repentance and intercession, it reaches back into the past with a healing hand.

King David was confronted by the sins of the past. In 2 Samuel 21, we learn that the nation was suffering from an overlooked injustice that dated back an entire generation. King Saul had broken covenant with the Gibeonites, and he shed their blood instead of honoring a commitment made by their forefather Joshua. After three years of drought, it was revealed by God that there was bloodguilt on their hands, and He demanded a response from that generation. This passage is often cited by

Christian Native American leaders as an example that God is not okay with the broken treaties (covenants) between the U.S. government and tribes throughout the frontier. How many treaties did our leaders break with Native Americans? Answer: All of them. I have been deeply impacted by Christian Native leaders when they are asked the question, "What must be done to make things right?" They haven't asked for restitution. Instead, they have only asked for an official apology. Publicly acknowledge that it was wrong, ask forgiveness, and release healing to a generation still suffering.

The wrongs of the past are already done, and they can't be undone. However, the Dream King reserves the right to take what the enemy meant for evil and use it for good. He is the God of the alternate ending—one that the devil can't foresee. God, in partnership with his people, has the ability to look to the past and remove obstacles where the blessings have been dammed up. When we touch those things in a repentant posture, the blessings begin to be released like a pent-up flood, and we know that God's love extends to a thousand generations (Deu. 7:9). Let those healing waters be released!

Even some in the United States Congress have sought to come to terms with the wrongs of the past. In 2008, a white lawmaker serving a black majority district in Memphis introduced a resolution that passed in the House of Representatives, apologizing to African-Americans for slavery and Jim Crow laws. This congressman appealed to his colleagues, saying:

> The fact is, slavery and Jim Crow are stains upon what is the greatest nation on the face of the earth and the greatest government ever conceived by man. But when

we conceived this government and said all men were created equal we didn't in fact make all men equal…We have
worked to form a more perfect union, and part of forming
a more perfect union is laws, and part of it is such as res-
olutions like we have before us today where we face up to
our mistakes and we apologize, as anyone should apologize for things that were done in the past that were wrong.
And we begin a dialogue that will hopefully lead us to a
better understanding of where we are in America today
and why certain conditions exist.[7]

The resolution stated:

African-Americans continue to suffer from the com-
plex interplay between slavery and Jim Crow—long after
both systems were formally abolished—through enormous damage and loss, both tangible and intangible,
including the loss of human dignity, the frustration of
careers and professional lives, and the long-term loss of
income and opportunity.[8]

The resolution concluded with words that, I believe, should
be preached from pulpits all across America:

An apology for centuries of brutal dehumanization and
injustices cannot erase the past, but confession of the
wrongs committed can speed racial healing and reconciliation and help Americans confront the ghosts of
their past.

How appropriate it was that this resolution originated in Tennessee's 9th District, home of the Lorraine Hotel where Rev. Martin Luther King, Jr. was assassinated. A concurrent resolution was passed by the Senate the following year, but it never made it to President Obama's desk for signature because no agreement could be made by lawmakers over language exempting the United States from any future claims of reparations by Black Americans.

That same year, Senator Sam Brownback of Kansas spearheaded a similar resolution that apologized to Native Americans for the injustice of the past. Sen. Brownback's groundbreaking efforts were the direct result of his dialog and partnership with prayer leaders—my friends and colleagues—working in this area of repentance and reconciliation. The House of Representatives passed a modified version of that effort, and it was eventually signed by President Obama. What an amazing testimony of God's conspicuous work beginning among his people and rising to touch the highest levels of government in the land. The only criticism that Native leaders had was that the President signed it without any fanfare, notoriety, or attention. Native Americans were left feeling as though the apology fell short of its potential because it functioned in form but failed in what should have been a more public display. Clearly, there is more work to be done.

UNSUNG HEROES

Once the lid was taken off my family history, it seemed as though there was no end to the extraordinary connections and discoveries I made. I started digging for more and more, and one day I had another unexpected encounter with the Dream King.

While sitting in the prayer room one day, I sensed the Lord speaking to my heart very clearly, "I want you to look at the relationship between the revival and the Revolution." Those were trigger words for me, and I instantly knew how to direct my attention. I began to look back to the 18th century.

This land has experienced several very significant moves of God in the form of revivals. Some have been so large in scale that we call them "great awakenings." The First Great Awakening occurred in the 1730s and 1740s and included recognizable preachers like Jonathan Edwards and George Whitfield, a close colleague of John Wesley. It was due to the preaching of Wesley in England that a young man named Francis Asbury came to the American colonies as a missionary in 1771. He brought Wesley's brand of "circuit rider" preaching to the new world.

As Methodism grew and the itinerant circuit riders swelled in ranks, the colonies were beginning to boil. Philosophical differences between Britain and her thirteen colonies reached a tipping point, and war erupted in 1775. A declaration of independence followed on July 4, 1776. The land was experiencing revival and revolution at the same time, which is where the Lord was directing my attention. Something curious was common to these two dimensions of revival and revolution that many would overlook. In the midst of both, God was speaking about the ending of slavery.

Quakers had taken a strong stance for the abolition of the slave trade. American Methodism had been born, and Rev. Francis Asbury was its spiritual father. Asbury was confronted by the evil of slavery that surrounded him as he crisscrossed the land. He reflected in his journal on June 10, 1778:

I find the more pious part of the people called Quakers, are exerting themselves for the liberation of the slaves. This is a very laudable design; and what the Methodists must come to, or, I fear, the Lord will depart from them.[9]

Asbury understood that, though the revival was great and Methodism was growing exponentially, a failure to rightly address the issue of slavery would hinder the advance of the Gospel. The abolitionist influence was growing in the colonies, and it soon found a champion among the Methodists. In the Conference of 1780, the Methodists took their first official action on the issue of slavery. The question was asked, "Ought not this Conference to require those traveling preachers who hold slaves to give promises to set them free?" With the weight of binding ordinance, the answer was given, "Yes."[10] This was a line drawn in the sand for righteousness. In the decades that followed, this rule would be challenged as pro-slavery sentiment pushed back in the South. Ministers refusing to emancipate their slaves were removed from membership.

The Methodist circuit rider was a conspicuous figure during the formation of the United States. His sober and serious demeanor served as a stark reminder of the unsaved soul's peril. Historian Matthew Simpson wrote, "To no other man does American civilization owe so much as to Bishop Asbury. He is worthy of a place among the heroes of '76."[11] While the founding forefathers were fighting for America's freedom from Britain, Asbury was fighting for her soul. Part of that fight included an uncompromising call for her to end slavery and provide freedom for all.

The most iconic symbol of the Methodist circuit rider was his saddlebags. In it was contained all his earthly belongings as he traveled relentlessly from place to place. Inside, you would find a Bible and hymn books, but there was another item to which we must pay careful attention. Manumission papers were also carried in the precious cargo. Manumission was the act of legally setting free slaves. Asbury and his circuit riders would preach the Gospel of salvation, and at the same time appeal for the newly-saved to set their slaves free. The free African-American population swelled from 32,000 in 1790 to 108,000 in 1810.[12] The effect of the Methodists on the growth of the abolitionist movement cannot be overstated. Everywhere you see the expansion of Methodism at that time in history, you find a massive increase in the population of freed slaves.

A few decades later, the nation was moving toward another great war, one bloodier than anyone could have ever anticipated. In spite of the revivals, even the Methodists ultimately separated north and south over the issue of slavery in 1844. It was an ominous foreshadowing of the split that would almost tear the entire nation apart sixteen years later.

ANOTHER UNEXPECTED DISCOVERY

I'm thankful for the abolitionist voices that took an unpopular stand in their day. At the very beginning of the nation, we see that it was the Christians leading the parade of history as they appealed to their countrymen on behalf of the suffering African. One highly-esteemed itinerant raised up in the New World was Rev. Philip Gatch, a friend of Rev. Asbury. He embodied all the best qualities of the Methodist circuit rider preachers with his steadfast endurance and abolitionist convictions. When he inherited nine slaves through marriage, it was recorded that he emancipated them all in 1788, stating in the contract:

> Know all men by these presents, that I, Philip Gatch, of Powhatan county [Virginia], do believe that all men are by nature equally free; and from a clear conviction of the injustice of depriving my fellow creatures of their natural rights, do hereby emancipate, or set free, the following persons.[13]

These circuit rider preachers appealed to the conscience of people right at a time when their foremost leaders were pondering certain unalienable rights derived by their Creator. Journals record that Rev. Asbury called upon George Washington in his home at Mount Vernon.[14] His appeal was for Washington's support and signature on a petition for the emancipation of slaves in Virginia. The founding forefathers had heated debates over the slavery issue, but abolitionist efforts ultimately failed at that time. Thomas Jefferson said of slavery, "We have the wolf by the ear, and we can neither hold him, nor safely let him go. Justice is in one scale, and self-preservation in the other."[15] Like a can kicked down the road, the consequences of their decisions would be handed to a future generation. America wanted her independence from oppression, yet she seemed to miss the irony that it would be wrought on the backs of African slaves.

As I was reading about the abolitionist efforts of Asbury, Gatch, and other circuit riders, I was led by the Lord to read a specific book that chronicled Methodist activity in Virginia. In it, I unexpectedly came across a piece of history that utterly stunned me. Rev. Gatch had been assigned to a circuit in central Virginia, but his health began to fail due to persecutions. He became a farmer and local preacher in Powhatan County as the Revolutionary War was in full swing. That area is very near where the Lockett homestead was located. The historical account stated:

> There are no records of extensive revivals in Virginia during the years 1779 and 1780. The war was fiercely raging in the South; the country was filled with alarms and the marching and counter-marching of armed men, kept the people in a constant state of excitement. There were gracious visitations, however, in some localities. Gatch mentions a revival of much interest in Powhatan County. It was felt with power among Methodists and Baptists. The ranks of the itinerancy received several valuable accessions from this work. Daniel Asbury, Lewis Chastain, Richard Tope, Bennett Maxey and Daniel Lockett, joined the Conference.[16]

When I read the name "Daniel Lockett" in the list of circuit riders, I was beside myself. I quickly pulled out my newly discovered family tree and began to scour through the lines. Right there, exactly where he should be in the genealogy, was Daniel Lockett. One of my ancestors was a Methodist circuit rider. Not only that, but he became one at a time when they were a band of uncompromising abolitionists.

Remember how I opened this chapter? We have all done things we regret, and we all share a bloody history that we've tried to forget. The enemy of our souls would have the failures of our past dominate our storylines and choke our individual and collective destinies. Yes, I have an ancestor who was the slave owner of Will's family. It's a tragic fact. But when I look back a little further to the previous generation, I find someone who was a revivalist and an abolitionist. So, the question I was faced with is what storyline did I want to be a part of? The blessing or the curse—the healing or the hurt?

I have chosen to have the story of blessing and healing be the driving force of my life.

My storyline is guided by the Dream King who has supernaturally brought me into a stream of revival and abolition. I choose to break the pattern of curses that may have been a part of my past. Instead, I choose life. My family and my future generations will walk in the path of Daniel Lockett. We will preach a Gospel of salvation through Jesus Christ, and we will labor for the freedom of many. Freedom for those oppressed by systemic injustice. Freedom for the most innocent in the womb.

Take a moment to ponder this. Leave it to God to answer the secret prayers of slaves by ending the American Civil War in the front yard of the family who had owned them. But because He's the God of the past, present, and future, he connected two brothers from those same two families to war against a new injustice in their day. In the process, he uncovered a hidden history of revival and abolition, and he made it abundantly clear that he's the author and finisher of our faith.

Who wouldn't want to serve this God? Who wouldn't want to be a part of the stories that he writes? Who wouldn't want to receive a divine reversal of their bad choices and worst regrets? The opportunity is before you right now. The Dream King wants to tell his story through you.

Chapter 7

BECOMING THE DREAM

Matt speaking:

We are all now faced with some hard decisions to make. What storyline do you want to be a part of? The healing or the hurt? The blessing or the curse? I want to share a powerful example of what can happen when you choose to interrupt the course of curses and, instead, branch off into blessings. There remains one last thing to reveal in this story about my life and Will's being woven together so extraordinarily. It begins back on a farm that was part of that Lockett homestead in Virginia. Remember from Chapter 5 that it was illegal for slaves to learn how to read and write throughout the South, and the whites who attempted to teach them were punished. Even after the Civil War and slavery had ended, it still wasn't popular to teach African Americans how to read and write. Therefore, in some cases, the legacy of secret meetings continued as the nation went into a time of transition during the Reconstruction years.

PAVING THE WAY FOR BLESSING

The autobiography of Robert Russa Moton records one such secret moment. Robert was born in 1867, just two years after the war had ended. His father was a hired hand on a Virginia plantation in Prince Edward County, where his mother was a cook. They lived near the big house working for Miss Lucy Lockett Vaughan. Moton wrote:

> About this time a rather interesting incident happened. While my work was new, my mother made me devote an hour at night to my blue-backed Holmes's Primer. She was my teacher, being one of the very few coloured women in our neighbourhood who could read at all. There was a popular belief that the Vaughans, notwithstanding their kindness and aristocratic ideas, objected to and opposed Negroes' reading and writing. My mother was very careful, therefore, that they should not know that she was teaching me to read, or even that she herself could read. For several years she had kept from them the fact that she even knew one letter of the alphabet from another, but one night after the day's work was done there was a gentle rap at the door of our two-roomed house. I remember that we were sitting before a big, open fire—my father, my mother, and I—my mother teaching me by the light from the fire. As the custom was in those days my mother called out to learn who was there. Imagine our consternation when the answer came back: "Miss Lucy." My mother was tempted to hide the book when she discovered who was at the door, but my father objected ... So

124

the door was opened and in walked "Miss Lucy" to find us in the very act.

Moton went on to describe the surprise of everyone when Lucy Lockett chose a different path of compassion and understanding in what turned out to be a historic moment:

She expressed the greatest surprise when she discovered what was taking place, but she astonished us equally when she indicated that she was very much pleased, and commended my mother on the fact that she could read and told her she was very wise to teach her son to read. The next day we were even more astonished and of course pleased when Miss Mollie, her youngest daughter, said to my mother that Mrs. Vaughan had asked her to give me a lesson for one hour every afternoon and to do the same for my mother if my mother would care to have her do so. So the next time my father went to Farmville, eight miles away, he bought the necessary books both for my mother and me, and my lessons began in a more systematic way with Miss Mollie as teacher and my mother as my "classmate" for one hour each afternoon.[1]

Moton recorded a beautiful sentiment when he reflected on the life of Lucy Lockett Vaughan after she died. He revealed:

Mrs. Vaughan, like her husband, possessed a very beautiful character and was beloved of everybody on the plantation. While I did not then appreciate the full gravity of the situation, I wept along with the others; for in spite of my youth I realized somewhat the loss that this death was to me as well as to others. For there was not a family on the plantation and scarcely a person who had not at some time been helped by her kindly personal attention to their needs and difficulties.[2]

It is profoundly significant that Lucy Lockett oversaw the tutoring of Robert Moton. He went on to become President of Tuskegee Institute after the death of Booker T. Washington. He was an educational advisor to legislators, and, in 1922, Moton delivered the dedication speech of the Lincoln Memorial in Washington, DC.

Just think of it. Lucy Lockett could have given in to the lingering social norms of her times and chosen a different and darker path. Perhaps young Robert's parents would have left that place in response, thereby altering the course of events in Robert's young life. Maybe he still would have gone on to greatness, but perhaps he wouldn't have under different conditions. While it's pointless to speculate what might have happened, what matters is that Miss Lucy chose a path of healing that interrupted the curses of the past and paved the way for blessings to flow.

The result was that Robert Moton, motivated in part by Miss Lucy's kindness, found himself standing on the steps of the Lincoln Memorial, commemorating the Emancipator and all those like him. On that same spot, Dr. Martin Luther King, Jr. stood 41 years later, declaring, "I have a dream that one day the sons of former slaves and the sons of former slave owners will be able to sit down together at the table of brotherhood." Another 41 years later, where else should Will and I meet but there? The Dream King had been at work all along, weaving and crafting an intricate storyline rich with hope and reconciliation.

Robert Russa Moton giving the dedication speech for the Lincoln Memorial, 1922.
Photo: Library of Congress[B]

RESTORING AMERICA'S FABRIC

In his keynote speech at the Lincoln Memorial on May 30, 1922, Robert Moton painted a stunning picture of America's earliest days that called into question an overly idealistic view of our origins:

But at the same time, another influence was working within the nation. While the Mayflower was riding at anchor preparing for her voyage from Plymouth, another ship had already arrived at Jamestown. The first was to bear the pioneers of freedom, freedom of thought and

127

freedom of conscience; the latter had already borne the pioneers of bondage, a bondage degrading alike to body, mind and spirit. Here then, upon American soil within a year, met the two great forces that were to shape the destiny of the nation. They developed side by side. Freedom was the great compelling force that dominated all, and like a great and shining light, beckoned the oppressed of every nation to the hospitality of these shores. But slavery like a brittle thread was woven year by year into the fabric of the nation's life.[3]

With these two realities of blessing and curse coexisting in the same storyline, Moton was right in highlighting that God, in His providence, was not content to leave things alone. In fact, he understood that it was God who was behind the conflict that brought resolution to the contradiction of freedom, and it was God who brought forth countercultural deliverers who paved the way. Moton explained:

In the process of time, as was inevitable, these great forces, the forces of liberty and the forces of bondage, from the ships at Plymouth and Jamestown, met in open conflict upon the field of battle. And how strange it is, through the same over-ruling Providence, that children of those who bought and sold their fellows into bondage should be among those who cast aside ties of language, of race, of religion and even of kinship, in order that a people not of their own race, or primarily of their own creed or color, but sharing a common humanity, should have the same measure of liberty and freedom which they themselves enjoyed.[4]

The Dream King is still in the business of raising up deliverers, whether it's men like the stuttering Moses or the eloquent Frederick Douglass. Jael was a woman who delivered her people with a tent peg (see Judg. 4:17-22) and Harriet Beecher Stowe was a woman who delivered the people with a pen. These examples prove that all of us are eligible to partner with Him in this great work to break the curses and unleash the blessings God intends for our nation. I believe an entire generation has been born for this divine purpose—to partner with God to usher in revival, to break systemic racism, and to fiercely protect the most vulnerable among us.

ANOTHER GREAT SURRENDER

Like slavery, abortion is also a brittle thread that has been woven year by year into the fabric of the nation's life. Parallel to the mistakes of the past, those who would desire better lives for themselves and the disadvantaged, today would do so by denying life to the weakest among us. There is no one more powerless, none more disenfranchised than the baby in the womb, who has no voice to defend herself or himself. The dream about the Appomattox Room discussed in Chapter 4 reveals God's intense desire for abortion to end. However, after decades of legalized abortion in America, this practice is interwoven into nearly every facet of society. To pull on this brittle scarlet thread seems to threaten an unraveling of American life as we know it. Regardless of this fear, we must consider that God would be behind such an unraveling. Etched in the stone of his memorial in Washington, DC, are the words of Abraham Lincoln's Second Inaugural Address. No doubt, Moton read them and, before beginning his own keynote address, gave an agreeing nod to Lincoln's immortal words:

If we shall suppose that American slavery is one of those offenses which, in the providence of God, must needs come, but which, having continued through His appointed time, He now wills to remove, and that He gives to both North and South this terrible war as the woe due to those by whom the offense came, shall we discern therein any departure from those divine attributes which the believers in a living God always ascribe to Him? Fondly do we hope, fervently do we pray, that this mighty scourge of war may speedily pass away. Yet, if God wills that it continue until all the wealth piled by the bondsman's two hundred and fifty years of unrequited toil shall be sunk, and until every drop of blood drawn with the lash shall be paid by another drawn with the sword, as was said three thousand years ago, so still it must be said, "The judgments of the Lord are true and righteous altogether."[5]

Many believe that abortion law is settled law. We would do well to remember that the same thing was said of earlier laws that once established and protected slavery. The same Dream King who reversed *Dred Scott* can reverse *Roe v. Wade*. Revival came. Hearts changed, and unjust laws changed, too. Just like the picture of General Lee signing unconditional surrender at Appomattox Court House, I believe another great surrender is coming to America. O, that we would surrender our will to His and step into divine blessing that touches a thousand generations.

A HOUSE OF HEALING

Our story took an interesting turn when I discovered that the end of the American Civil War was uniquely connected to my family. The scene of General Lee's last battle at Lockett's Farm gives us stunning language that helps us understand the moment we're in now. In my study of what happened on April 6, 1865, I came across the following description:

> While crossing Sailor's Creek below the Lockett Farm the traffic became so heavy that the bridge across the creek broke. This required Gordon's men to take a stand on a rise before the Lockett House as the wagon train piled up in the valley below. The event was witnessed by E. Lelia Lockett, then 18. She recalled, "The Confederate army formed a line of battle across the front yard…The cannon was planted on the hill, just in front of the house, facing the approaching Union army, which took a stand just in firing distance of the Confederate army, back of our house. The Confederate officer…advised my father to take his family in the basement, which was three feet in the ground, for safety, but if he could avoid it he would not shell the house." You can see the house was between the two armies.[6]

The Confederate army had gotten stuck in the mud, and they were forced to make a final stand. They were in the front yard, and the pursuing Union army emerged from the woods in the back yard. The Lockett house was all that stood between the two armies. Consider the following Biblical description given by the

131

prophet Ezekiel:

> And I sought for a man among them who should build up
> the wall and stand in the breach before me for the land, that
> I should not destroy it, but I found none. (Ezekiel 22:30)

That image of the Lockett house in between the warring armies is a powerful picture of this kind of prayer and intercession. God wants a house that stands in between the brothers trying to rip each other apart. Just like the Lockett's physical house still bears the bullet holes and battle scars from that day of battle, we too are bound to take some shots if we dare to be in that controversial place. Some wounds might even leave scars, but the benefits are worth the sacrifice if they bring the unity that we've sought for so long. I want to be a part of that house; don't you?

Another interesting aspect is described of the scene after the battle ended. Lelia Lockett recalled:

> The Union army camped on the field for the night. They
> built their campfires far and near, and cooked a sump-
> tuous supper, which they were generous enough to share
> with us, as we have been too busy all day cooking and
> feeding our half-starved soldiers to take time to eat...
> The wounded soldiers [of both armies] were brought
> in our house which was used for a hospital, and taken
> care of by Union surgeons, until they could be moved or
> died...Also helping to nurse the soldiers were two Afri-
> can-Americans at the Lockett home identified as Branch
> and Henry Booker.[7]

The wooden floorboards of the Lockett house were said to have been stained with the blood of both North and South. Likewise, we are called to be a place of healing for everyone. Though our skin color may be different, all of our blood is red. God is no discriminator of the disabled. He is no segregator of the sick. I find it fascinating that history records that a young African American boy named Branch was there and helped to nurse the wounded. What a noteworthy name considering the Old Testament prophets referred to Jesus as the Branch (see Isa. 11:1, Jer. 23:5, Jer. 33:15, Zec. 3:8, Zec 6:12). It speaks to me that Jesus wants to get his hands dirty by being right in the middle of our mess, bringing healing to everyone.

Will speaking:

Matt just reminded me of listening to many preachers who have said, "God has a way of taking our mess, to make His message." I mention this because many historians of the Civil Rights Movement report that Dr. King received part of his inspiration for his speech from a prayer in the middle of a mess. In 1962 Dr. King went to Terrell County, Georgia, to speak at Mt. Olive Baptist Church. The Ku Klux Klan had recently burned the church down. Prathia Hall, a 22-year-old college student and member of SNCC (Student Non-Violent Coordinating Committee) was invited to pray as part of the service. During Hall's prayer she used the phrase, "I have a dream." Jae Jones reports:

Hall was the daughter of Rev. Berkeley Hall, a Baptist minister, and was known for her oratory skills. Through her prayer, she shared her vision of what she hoped for the future of Black Americans. In her prayer, she used the phrase, "I have a dream" many times. Dr. King was very impressed with Prathia's prayer. In particular, he admired her use of the phrase, "I have a dream." As ministers often do, King would later incorporate, "I have a dream" into some of his own speeches. By late 1962, the phrase was reported to have been a regular part of King's sermons.[8]

While the origin of Dr. King's inspiration for the phrase, "I have a dream" has been debated, what has been verified is that Prathia Hall used the phrase in prayer before Dr. King made it popular in his speech on August 28, 1963, in Washington. It is amazing that in the middle of a mess created by hatred, Prathia Hall caught the Dream King's revelation for hope in the midst of prayer. In the same way that there was a Lockett house that stood in the gap, and Dr. King and other Civil Rights leaders were inspired to carry on through their prayer meetings, God is calling a new generation to stand in the gap as members in His house of prayer. The prophet Jeremiah decreed, "Therefore, thus says the LORD, 'If you return, then I will restore you— Before Me you will stand; and if you extract the precious from the worthless, you will become My spokesman'" (Jeremiah 15:19 NASB). By extracting this "I have a dream" prayer from worthless rubble caused by the hatred of the Ku Klux Klan, Dr. King became God's spokesman. To use his words, "out of the mountain of despair, a stone of hope"[9] emerged in the form of a speech.

I don't think it was an accident that Matt and I were led to the Lincoln Memorial to find one another in a prayer meeting on Martin Luther King, Jr. Day. I believe we are all going to find each other in the prayer meetings. We will truly find each other as hope arises. In those divine moments, we'll see clearly that, "red and yellow, black and white, they are precious in His sight."[10] It's in the prayer meetings that we'll get God's perspective, and he'll give us His love for one another.

Do you know that Jesus commanded us to love our enemies? That's easier said than done. Love for your enemy doesn't come naturally, and it never happens instantaneously. How is it even possible? In the Sermon on the Mount, Jesus said, "But I say to you, love your enemies and pray for those who persecute you, so that you may be sons of your Father who is in heaven" (Matthew 5:44). We cannot overlook prayer as the key. Love for your enemies is possible when you pray for them—not just once but continually. Do you pray for those whom you perceive to hate you? How often do you consider the needs of those you feel want to do you harm? Try as we might, I don't think any of us gets to sidestep this holy command. In prayer, hope replaces despair, and love drives out hatred. Never forget that Jesus cried out on behalf of his torturers with his dying breaths.

THE TABLE OF BROTHERHOOD

Dr. King said that he dreamed of sons of former slaves and slave owners sitting down together at the table of brotherhood. One of the profound things that happened with me in our story, after all the excitement wore off, took place when the realization settled in that Matt's family actually owned my family. At times, while processing our initial discovery, I was not only searching through genealogical records, I was also searching for healing. I find it interesting that before Matt and I learned about Daniel Lockett, the abolitionist preacher fighting against slavery, we first had to wrestle with the fact that Matt's family owned my family. We didn't learn about Daniel Lockett until over a year later. Once the excitement of our initial story and God connection wore off, I had to wrestle with thoughts, attitudes, and emotions connected to painful stories passed down in my family related to slavery. After sharing my story for years before I met Matt and carrying the kettle used for prayer by my slave forefathers around the country, suddenly I had a face to connect with all the painful memories of slave stories passed down in my family, and the irony is that face belonged to one of my dearest friends. Matt and I talked about and prayed through some of this, and some of it I did alone. Let me be clear: there is no restitution my family desires, nor do I feel Matt owes me any debt.

After a decade of friendship and sitting at the table of brotherhood in a conciliatory relationship, I realized I had more things to reconcile in my own heart. This wasn't anything overwhelming, but it was something I needed to address, and I forgave: I forgave the Locketts for owning my family. I also forgave them for the painful story of my forefather, Uncle Willie, who was beaten to death.

After more than a decade of friendship and ministry partnership through sharing our story together, I can attest that God has done a deep work of forgiveness in my heart. I have forgiven Matt's family, but not only that—we have chosen to walk together as covenant brothers in Christ. Not only have I embraced forgiveness, but I've also embraced the abolitionist zeal of Daniel Lockett, who was a voice for the voiceless during slavery. Even more, we have come to embrace the Lockett name.

During the time we found the history of our families, my wife was pregnant. Convinced we were having a girl and settling on girl names, we were surprised to discover we were having a boy. We prayed and came up with the name Samuel Ford. I then remembered something my grandparents told me. My grandfather, William Ford Sr., was born Lawrence Locket. His mother Nora died young, and his grandparents, Levi and Harriet Locket, who were born just as slavery was ending, raised him. I was told that they didn't want him to have the slave surname of Locket, so his first and last names were changed to the names of two family friends, and my grandfather was renamed William Lawrence Ford. Seeing the powerful way that God had connected my family and Matt's, my wife and I chose to redeem the Locket name and history by naming our son Samuel Locket Ford. When I called Matt to let him know what we planned to name our son and connect to the redemptive storyline of the Locketts, he was overwhelmed because his youngest son is also named Samuel Lockett.

Matt and I have experienced a lot at this table of brotherhood. We have laughed at the table of brotherhood (we both share quick-witted humor and fun), celebrated at the table of brotherhood (our first-born children are both daughters who share the same birthday, and we both have four children), eaten at the table of brotherhood (we have even shared Thanksgiving together), and wept together at the table of brotherhood (both our parents have passed away, and our mothers died on the same day of the year). Now I sit across from him at the table of brotherhood, able to look into the eyes of my friend, forgiving and laying aside the fact that his family was ever my enemy. The mutual love and respect we have for one another has drained the power of past hurt and pain.

Our shared focus is on connecting to God's storyline of healing for our nation by praying together at the table of brotherhood. We believe our profoundly unique set of circumstances and their providential orchestration reveal the heart of a loving God, the Dream King Himself, who is calling us all to the table of brotherhood. Oh, America, there is still room at this table. Matt and I don't believe it's a coincidence that we met first in a prayer meeting on Martin Luther King, Jr. Day at the Lincoln Memorial and have been sitting at the table of brotherhood ever since. Today, he and I endeavor to stand united in the house of prayer to heal a divided nation once again. Now God is using us to call believers of all races to unite in prayer and intercession because only a united church can heal a divided nation.

We do this by connecting to the unfinished business of the past in a meaningful way. On April 9, 2016, Matt and I participated in a prayer service called United Cry, held at the Lincoln Memorial. April 9, of course, was the anniversary of the Civil War's end, and it also happens to be the day Dr. King was buried. Perhaps this date represents the seed of renewal going into the ground. Bishop Harry Jackson helped to assemble many notable people to be a part of the gathering, including Dr. Alveda King (King's niece), Dr. Bernice King (King's daughter), Lynn Jackson (great-great-grand-daughter of Dred Scott), and Bill Haley, Jr (grandson of Alex Haley, author of *Roots*).

For the first time, Matt and I brought the kettle to the place where we had met years earlier. On this occasion the kettle was filled with water, and we used it to wash the feet of the King family along with the others. We did this in the same spirit as when Jesus washed the feet of his disciples to demonstrate to them his humility and his identity as a servant (John 13:1-17).

We repented for mistakes made in the past and for those in the Church who did not pick up King's God-given dream to fight for justice, unity, and love. They graciously received this act of repentance and extended forgiveness for the healing of the nation. Matt and I were moved to tears as we also washed one another's feet.

Then something very significant happened. Bishop Harry Jackson, who leads a coalition called The Reconciled Church, presented to several leaders the Mantle of Destiny award, provided by The King Family Legacy Foundation. This honor recognizes leaders working to bring healing to the racial issue in America. Recipients were charged to make disciples, and the King family prayed for them to continue the unfinished work of Dr. King. That moment was a prophetic sign that God was releasing a new spiritual mantle. However, it's not for just a few people—it's for all of us.

In December, 2017, the clergy in Charlottesville, Virginia, asked us to participate in a prayer meeting for healing the community, following the racist violence that had occurred a few months earlier. Not far from that meeting stands Lockett's farmhouse, where a memorial stone in the front yard reads: "Here Lee Fought His Last Battle, April 6th, 1865." I cannot tell you how profound it was to stand together at the house that united us, which had also once stood between a divided nation. It's hard to describe the sense of awe, knowing that prayers from Christian Lockett slaves and abolitionist circuit riders were literally answered in this front yard. My family's 200-year-old kettle pot in hand, Matt and I went back to the spot where the prayers underneath the kettle were answered. In essence, we built an altar there and prayed. Though we prayed with tears of joy in

Will Ford and Matt Lockett carrying the kettle to the Lockett farmhouse.

thankfulness, we also prayed for another laying down of arms between divided Americans. Our earnest prayer is that another unconditional surrender would come to this nation again.

IT'S TIME TO DREAM AGAIN

Dr. King's *I Have A Dream* speech is easily one of the most powerful and memorable speeches in human history. We revere this Nobel Peace Prize winner for his heart of compassion that drove him to inspire unity and equality. No doubt, Dr. King knew his dream was an expression of the dream of the King of kings, Jesus Christ, the Dream King, and that what He prayed for us in John 17 has the potential to change the world as we know it. He prayed that we would be one, so that His glory would come and the world would believe God is real and is involved in our lives.

God has encouraged me along the way with more dreams.

My wife's friend, Mary Wells, had a powerful dream that she shared with me. Mary is from England, and though we had never met before, she told me the night before we met that she had been introduced to me in a dream. She said, "I don't dream often, but when I do, it is usually very significant. I dreamed that you introduced yourself to me, and handed me a book written by Martin Luther King, Jr. You told me that Dr. King dedicated chapter 17 of the book to you. I turned to that chapter, and Dr. King nicknamed you "John," and he thanked you for taking up his unfinished business." What's interesting is that Mary knew nothing of my story with Matt, nor did she know about my Dr. King dream (detailed in Chapter 1). It's telling that in her dream, I was nicknamed John, in chapter 17 of the book.

The Dream King Himself was encouraging us that we still have unfinished business. Our Heavenly Father is still answering the prayer of His son from John 17, where Jesus prayed that we would be one, so His glory could come so that the world would believe in Him.

THIS IS A STORY FOR RIGHT NOW

Matt and Will speaking together at the table of brotherhood:

In 2001, former Kansas Senator Sam Brownback was inspired to work on a resolution for the creation of a Smithsonian National Museum of African American History and Culture for the National Mall. For decades, similar ideas had languished in bureaucracy and controversy. This work, carried out in partnership with Georgia Congressman John Lewis, garnered a lot of attention. During that time, *CBS News* conducted an interview with Senator Brownback, and they asked him what he would put in a museum like that. Part of Brownback's inspiration emerged in his response when he explained that he had recently heard the story of slaves who secretly prayed for freedom underneath an old kettle pot. He had heard Will share the story of his ancestors and was deeply moved. The Senator said he thought something like that would be good for the museum and for the nation.

Gripped by the story of the kettle, the interviewers filmed a studio interview with Will to hear the strange story of secret prayer. Soon afterwards, it was due to air, but then the terrorist attacks of September 11 occurred. In the media frenzy, Will's interview about the kettle never saw the light of day. It was as though God had put his finger on the pause button for the public sharing of the story. Years passed, and the story of the kettle was shared around the nation in churches and small settings. In the meantime, President George W. Bush authorized construction of the African American museum in 2003, and its grand opening was in September 2016. Those additional 15 years allowed the story to mature and develop in its entirety, now including the backdrop of Matt's family. Now it seems God is taking His finger off the pause button. This story was meant to be told right now, and America needs it now more than ever before.

DO THE DREAM

We must all imagine being the ones who become the answer to Jesus' prayer. When we intentionally pursue unity as God desires, the petty mindsets that continually bring division fall in our midst, and the glory of God comes in power. What once seemed impossible, suddenly becomes possible. When we reject the stereotypes used by the devil to keep us apart, the glory of God comes and fills us with love and understanding for one another. Divine purposes and God-ordained destinies then have our attention more than the color of someone's skin.

When our relationships with each other demonstrate forgiveness and are free of prejudice, we get the fullness of what Jesus wanted: the world will believe in Him. When we can live as one, then the Dream King is on full display in all His splendor and majesty, carefully weaving a redemptive story through human beings who would otherwise hate each other. Jesus knew there could be no more persuasive argument made to convince people that He is Who He says He is than transformed human minds and hearts loving God and loving each other.

We have a dream that one day soon, the sons and daughters of a divided nation will behold the glory of the Lord and believe that Jesus Christ, the Dream King, is alive, loves them, and has come to set them free and make us one.

God cares deeply about injustice, contrary to what many think. The Bible teaches that where there is oppression, the unjust treatment of people groups, or the senseless loss of human life, there is a cry that God hears, and it has His undivided attention. Can we hear that same cry? It is in this generation's spiritual DNA to respond to that call for help. Thankfully, we don't have to do it alone or solve it by uninspired means. It begins with the revelation that Jesus Christ has already made a way. Hebrews 12:24 says that the blood of Jesus speaks a better word than the blood of those who have been mistreated and murdered. The power is at hand for Christians to be the remedy for the sickness afflicting America and the nations of the earth.

Through the power of forgiveness, the past can be redeemed. By Christ's stripes (see Isa. 53:5), history's wounds can be healed, and by the precious blood of Jesus, we are united in a bond that transcends class and racial division. By design, God has made us to do it together, loving each other and loving Him at the table of brotherhood. We still see a few empty seats. There is still room at the table. Come join us.

This is my story, this is my song,

praising my Savior all the day long.[11]

Rev. Dr. Martin Luther King, Jr., Photo: Library of Congress[C]

If God is a dreamer, which He is, and if He loves dreamers, which He does, then how precious to Him must be those who nurture dreams and dreamers. No mission more productive can be imagined than the raising up of dreamers. One who dreams his own dream does a a mighty thing. Those who empower and unleash an army of dreamers are the divine multiplicant of kingdom arithmetic.[12]

Mark Rutland, *Dream*

ENDNOTES

Chapter 1: Kettle Prayers

1. Colossians 3:22-25 says, "Slaves, in all things obey those who are your masters on earth, not with external service, as those who merely please men, but with sincerity of heart, fearing the Lord. Whatever you do, do your work heartily, as for the Lord rather than for men, knowing that from the Lord you will receive the reward of the inheritance. It is the Lord Christ whom you serve. For he who does wrong will receive the consequences of the wrong which he has done, and that without partiality." In this letter, the apostle Paul was addressing indentured servants (a form of slavery under which someone becomes a slave for a specific period of time in order to pay a debt, which is radically different from slavery as it was practiced in America). Rather than being a salvation passage, Colossians 3: 22-25 deals with the moral conduct between believers in Colosse during the time of Paul's ministry.

Taken in context with the other verses of Colossians 3, we can see that Paul is addressing relationship issues in the church. In Colossians 3: 11, he even says there is neither slave nor free in Christ. Because we've surrendered our sinful identity (old self) as Christians, based on our identity in Christ (new self) we are to live out a moral conduct in all our relationships based on whom we belong to and whom we've become. Therefore, between husbands, wives, children, slaves, workers and masters, this is what your conduct will look like. During the time of slavery, Colossians 3: 22-25 was twisted and manipulated into a salvation passage, but it does not address salvation. The inheritance mentioned here is the reward believers gain for their faithfulness after salvation, not for salvation.

The last verse related to these relationships is for masters or slave owners, who are given a harsh reminder in Colossians 4: 1. The verse says, "Masters, grant to your slaves justice and fairness, knowing that you too have a Master in heaven." In other words, "Masters, realize that you are slaves to the Divine Master, and you will give an account some day." As evidenced by the Lord's treatment of the unjust master in Luke 12: 45, who was severely punished for treating the other slaves badly because he thought his master was delaying His appearing, we see that God did not approve of—nor will He ever approve of—cruel, inhumane treatment, including slavery in America. He desires for all people to be free (see John 8:36).

2. Abraham Lincoln, "Second Inaugural Address," https://www.loc.gov/item/mal4361300/, accessed January 22, 2018.

3. Martin Luther King, Jr., "I Have A Dream," August 28, 1963, https://www.archives.gov/files/press/exhibits/dream-speech.pdf, accessed February 25, 2018.

4. Martin Luther King, Jr., James Melvin Washington, *A Testament of Hope: The Essential Writings and Speeches of Martin Luther King, Jr.* (HarperOne, an imprint of HarperCollins Publishers, 2006) 217.

5. King, "I Have A Dream."

6. King, "I Have A Dream."

Chapter 2: Hidden History

1. Ronald F. Youngblood, F. F. Bruce, R. K. Harrison, *Nelson's Illustrated Bible Dictionary: New and Enhanced Edition* (Nashville: Thomas Nelson, 2014), Kindle edition.
2. Katherine Dixon Carter Blankenburg, *Thomas Lockett of Virginia: A Genealogical Memoir* (San Diego: Arts & Crafts Press, 1940), XIII.
3. Elizabeth Barrett Browning, *Aurora Leigh* (Hansebooks, 2016).
4. Ken Gire, *Windows of the Soul: Hearing God in the Everyday Moments of your Life* (Grand Rapids: Zondervan, 2017), 45.

Chapter 3: Poetry or Prophecy?

1. David Watson, *Called & Committed* (Wheaton: Harold Shaw Publishers, 1982), 83.
2. Year: 1870; Census Place: Sutton Plantation Ward 3, Carroll, Louisiana; Roll: M593_509; Page: 262A; Image: 41939; Family History Library Film: 552008, 1870 United States Federal Census, Ancestry.com, Operations, Inc., Date, 2009, Provo, UT.
3. King, "I Have A Dream."

Chapter 4: There Are No Accidents

1. Daniel G. Brinton, *The Basis of Social Relations; A Study In Ethnic Psychology*, (New York, G. P. Putnam's Sons, 1902), 133.
2. Pamela Newkirk, "When the Bronx Zoo exhibited a man in an iron cage," *CNN*, June 3, 2015, https://www.cnn.com/2015/06/03/opinions/newkirk-bronx-zoo-man-cage/index.html, accessed February 27, 2018.
3. Irin Carmon, "For eugenic sterilization victims, belated justice," *MSNBC*, June 27, 2014, http://www.msnbc.com/all/eugenic-sterilization-victims-belated-justice, accessed May 24, 2016.
4. Edwin Black, *War Against The Weak* (Washington, DC: Dialogue Press, 2012), 127.
5. Robert Wald Sussman, *The Myth of Race: The Troubling Persistence of an Unscientific Idea* (Cambridge: Harvard University Press, 2014), 91.
6. Ryan Bomberger, "The Mother of Planned Parenthood," The Radiance Foundation, http://www.toomanyaborted.com/sanger/, accessed February 8, 2018.
7. The United States has less than five percent of the world's population; however, it has almost 25 percent of the world's total prison population. The numbers today are much higher than they were 30 or 40 years ago despite the fact that crime is at historic lows. The overall prison population grew from 759,100 in 1980 to 1,179,200 by 1995. Today, the number is 2.4 million, with black men comprising 38% of the total prison population, yet only comprising 6% of the national population. A major contributing factor to this was pointed out in Michelle Alexander's book, *The New Jim Crow*, which reveals that a new permanent underclass has been created by those with felonies, who lose voting rights in most states, food assistance, and federal housing, creating a spiral of hopelessness. Some are making the case that beyond a new form of Jim Crow, this has become a new form of eugenic warehousing to control a population of people.

Chapter 5: Secret Sanctuaries

1. "Virginia's Slave Codes: 1705," *PBS Online*, http://www.pbs.org/wgbh/aia/part1/1p268.html, accessed August 16, 2017.

2. "Slavery and the Making of America," *Thirteen*, 2004, https://www.thirteen.org/wnet/slavery/experience/education/docs1.html, accessed December 17, 2017.

3. Moses Gandy, *Narrative of the Life of Moses Grandy, Late a Slave in the United States of America* (Chapel Hill: Docsouth Books), Kindle edition.

4. "Slave Narratives: Edd Roby," http://myfamily.com, accessed May 24, 2017.

5. Albert J. Raboteau, *Slave Religion: The Invisible Institution in the Antebellum South* (New York: Oxford University Press, 1978), 215.

6. Albert J. Raboteau, "The Secret Religion of the Slaves: They often risked floggings to worship God," *Christianity Today*, http://www.christianitytoday.com/history/issues/issue-33/secret-religion-of-slaves.html, accessed February 23, 2017.

7. "Slave Narratives: Laura Thornton," http://myfamily.com, accessed February 25, 2017.

8. Federal Writer's Project, United States Work Project Administration, "Born in Slavery: Slave Narratives from the Federal Writers' Project, 1936-1938: North Carolina Narratives," vol. 11, part 2, Alex Woods, http://memory.loc.gov/cgibin/ampage?collId=mesn&fileName=112/mesn112.db&recNum=417, accessed June 4, 2004.

9. Federal Writer's Project, United States Work Project Administration, "Born in Slavery: Slave Narratives from the Federal Writers' Project, 1936-1938, North Carolina Narratives," vol. 11, part 1, Kitty Hill, p. 425. http://memory.loc.gov/cgibin/ampage?collId=mesn&fileName=111/mesn111.db&recNum=425 (accessed June 4, 2004).

151

10. "Born in Slavery: Slave Narratives from the Federal Writers' Project, 1936-1938, Texas Narratives," vol. 16, part 1, Ex-Slave Stories, Texas, Ellen Butler, 177.

11. Raboteau, *Slave Religion: The Invisible Institution in the Antebellum South* (New York: Oxford University Press, 1978), 216.

12. James Washington, *Conversations with God: Two Centuries of Prayers by African Americans* (New York: HarperCollins Publishers, 1994), 51.

13. Dutch Sheets and William Ford III, *History Makers*, (Ada, Michigan: Baker Publishing Group, 2004), 102.

14. James Washington, *Conversations with God: Two Centuries of Prayers by African Americans* (New York: HarperCollins Publishers, 1994), 46.

15. George W. Bush, "Remarks by the President on Goree Island" (speech, Goree Island, Senegal, July 8, 2003), White House. http://www.whitehouse.gov/news/releases/2003/07/20030708-1.html (accessed June 8, 2004).

Chapter 6: What Storyline Do You Want To Be A Part Of?

1. John Wesley to William Wilberforce, February 24, 1791, "The Letters of John Wesley: 1791," Wesley Center Online, accessed December 15, 2017, http://wesley.nnu.edu/john-wesley/the-letters-of-john-wesley/wesleys-letters-1791/.

2. Soraya Nadia McDonald, "Ben Affleck's deleted 'Finding Your Roots' segment shows his Savannah ancestor owned 25 slaves," *The Washington Post*, April 23, 2015, https://www.washingtonpost.com/news/arts-and-entertainment/wp/2015/04/23/ben-afflecks-deleted-finding-your-roots-segment-shows-his-savannah-ancestor-owned-25-slaves/?utm_term=.b25e50341123, accessed October 12, 2017.

3. Matthew Henry, "Commentary on Matthew," Bible Gateway, https://www.biblegateway.com/resources/matthew-henry/Matt.23.13-Matt.23.33, accessed December 17, 2017.

4. Strong's H3415, *Blue Letter Bible*, https://www.blueletterbible.org/lang/lexicon/lexicon.cfm?Strongs=H3415&t=KJV, accessed January 8, 2018.

5. Strong's H8074, *Blue Letter Bible*, https://www.blueletterbible.org/lang/lexicon/lexicon.cfm?Strongs=H8074&t=KJV, accessed January 8, 2018.

6. "Dr. Martin Luther King's visit to Cornell College," Cornell College, http://news.cornellcollege.edu/dr-martin-luther-kings-visit-to-cornell-college/, accessed December 15, 2017.

7. Steve Cohen, "Congressman Cohen's Slavery Apology Resolution Passes the House of Representatives," July 29, 2008, https://cohen.house.gov/press-release/congressman-cohens-slavery-apology-resolution-passes-house-representatives.

8. "H.Res.194 - Apologizing for the enslavement and racial segregation of African-Americans," 110th Congress (2007-2008), https://www.congress.gov/bill/110th-congress/house-resolution/194/text, accessed October 12, 2017.

9. Francis Asbury, *Journal of Rev. Francis Asbury, Bishop of the Methodist Episcopal Church, from August 7, 1771, to December 7, 1815*, vol. 1, 3 vols. (New York: N. Bangs and T. Mason, 1821).

10. *Minutes of the Annual Conferences of the Methodist Episcopal Church, for the Years 1773 to 1828.* (New York: T. Mason and G. Lane, 1840), 12.

11. Matthew Simpson, *A Hundred Years of Methodism* (New York: Nelson & Phillips, 1876), 102.

12. John H. Wigger, *Taking Heaven by Storm* (New York: Oxford University Press, 1998), 137.

13. William W. Bennett, *Memorials of Methodism in Virginia: From Its Introduction Into the State, in the Year 1772, to the Year 1829* (Richmond: Published by the author, 1871), 133.

14. Thomas Coke, *Extracts of the Journals of the Rev. Dr. Coke's Five Visits to America* (London: G. Paramore, 1793), 45.

15. Thomas Jefferson to John Holmes, April 22, 1820, Library of Congress, https://www.loc.gov/exhibits/jefferson/159.html, accessed February 2, 2018.

16. Bennett, *Memorials of Methodism in Virginia*, 135.

Chapter 7: Becoming the Dream

1. Robert Russa Moton, *Finding a Way Out: An Autobiography* (Garden City: Doubleday, Page & Company, 1921), Chapter II, Kindle Edition.

2. Moton, *Finding a Way Out*.

3. Robert Russa Moton, "Address of Robert Russa Moton at the Dedication of the Lincoln Memorial, Washington, D.C., May 30th, 1922," https://memory.loc.gov/cgi-bin/ampage?collId=amrlm&fileName=mm01page.db&recNum=0&itemLink=r?ammem/AMALL:@field(NUMBER+@band(amrlm+mm01)), accessed August 16, 2017.

4. Moton, "Dedication of the Lincoln Memorial."

5. Lincoln, "Second Inaugural Address."

6. Greg Eanes, *The Battles of Sailor's Creek* (Burkeville: E & H Publishing Company, Inc., 2001), 149-150.

7. Eanes, *The Battles of Sailor's Creek*, 157.

8. Jae Jones, "Prathia Hall: Tough Platform Speaker Dr. Martin Luther King Preferred Not to Follow," Black Then, December 1, 2017, https://blackthen.com/prathia-hall-tough-platform-speaker-dr-martin-luther-king-preferred-not-to-follow/, accessed 2-28-2018. In researching the iconic phrase, "I Have A Dream," Drew Hansen gives other possibilities. Drew Hansen, *The Dream: Martin Luther King, Jr., and the Speech that Inspired a Nation* (New York: Harper Collins Publishers Inc., 2003).

9. King, "I Have A Dream."

10. Clare Herbert Woolston, *Jesus Loves the Little Children*, written to the tune of *Tramp, Tramp, Tramp, the Boys are Marching* by George Frederick Root, n.d.

11. Blessed Assurance, Lyrics by Fanny J. Crosby, 1873.

12. Mark Rutland, *Dream* (Lake Mary: Charisma House, 2003), 9.

Appendix of Images

A. *Ota Benga*, Prints & Photographs Division, [reproduction number, e.g., LC-B2-1234] (Washington: Library of Congress, 1906), https://www.loc.gov/item/2014702691/, accessed February 22, 2018.

B. *Dr. Moton, principal of the Tuscagee [sic] Inst. at the Lincoln Memorial dedication excercises [sic]*, (Washington: Library of Congress, 1922), https://www.loc.gov/item/90707742/, accessed February 22, 2018.

C. Don Rice, *Martin Luther King, Jr., half-length portrait, facing left, speaking at microphones, during anti-war demonstration, New York City*, in *World Journal Tribune* (Washington: Library of Congress, 1967), https://www.loc.gov/item/94505369/, accessed February 22, 2018.

For more about Will and Matt visit
DreamStreamCompany.com

WILL FORD is the Director of the Marketplace Leadership Major at Christ For The Nations Institute and is the co-founder of 818 The Sign. Many know him internationally, however, for his family heirloom passed down through history and its connection to slavery and prayer for freedom.

As a leader in the prayer movement, Will uses this "prayer bowl" as a catalyst for mobilizing prayer and teaching about intercession, revival, and societal transformation. He believes the prayers of a godly remnant of all races—revivalists and abolitionists—brought revival to America and ultimately ended slavery. Receiving their mantle from yesterday, Will is actively training a new generation to release justice to the most marginalized today. Will is a father of four. He and his wife Dehavilland reside in Dallas, TX.

MATT LOCKETT is the Executive Director of the Justice House of Prayer DC, located on Capitol Hill in Washington. From the governmental gate of the nation, Matt leads prayer and intercession that appeals to a holy hill higher than Capitol Hill—to a heavenly court above the Supreme Court.

Matt and his wife Kim have four children. They have served as full-time missionaries in the nation's capital since just after the founding of JHOP DC in 2004. Matt's passion is to help father a young, consecrated generation that will usher justice into the earth. Matt travels and speaks on the topics of prayer, fasting, governmental intercession, and racial reconciliation.

Matt also oversees Bound4LIFE, a pro-life prayer movement universally recognized by iconic red tape worn over the mouth with the word "LIFE" handwritten on it. "It's not a protest. It's a prayer meeting."

Learn more and get valuable
resources that will encourage
your prayer life

THE Sign

818 The Sign calls for a generation to embrace its spiritual identity through intimacy with Jesus. Our desire is to raise up a new generation of prophetic leaders by training them not only in the gifts of the spirit, but also in biblical righteousness and justice to tackle the issues facing the hour in which we live.

As a community, 818 The Sign is committed to healing the racial divide by bringing the body of Christ together. We provide a vision of unity through diversity under the banner of love, forgiveness, and collective synergy in response to Jesus' prayer in John 17, that we would be one, so His glory would come, so that the world would believe. We believe that based on this passage, one of the greatest signs and wonders to the world is unity through diversity in the church.

818thesign.org

JUSTICE HOUSE OF PRAYER DC

Justice House of Prayer DC is an evangelical missions organization serving Washington, DC and the nation through ongoing prayer and strategic activism. JHOP DC is committed to pray for national leaders and seeking spiritual transformation and cultural reformation established from the governmental gate of the nation's capital.

In the spirit of day and night prayer, JHOP DC operates a prayer room open to the public and conducts regular times of teaching and training for interns and the local body of Christ.

JHOPDC.com

BOUND4LIFE

Bound4LIFE is a grassroots movement created to pray for the ending of abortion, carry the spirit of adoption, and ignite revival and reformation. The mission is to mobilize a massive surge of prayer through two simple ways to engage:

Silent Sieges—Public stands of silent prayer wearing "Life Tape" in front of courthouses and abortion centers around the nation

Life Bands—Millions of Christians wearing red wristbands engraved with the word LIFE. Those who wear the Life Band make a three-part commitment to:
- Pray daily for the ending of abortion
- Vote for candidates and policies that are pro-life
- Obey God in acts of compassion and justice

This movement is universally recognized by red tape worn over the mouth with the word "LIFE" handwritten on it. It is not a protest—it is a silent prayer meeting. You can be a part of this movement now and start a Bound4LIFE Chapter right where you live.

Bound4LIFE.com

Other books by the authors

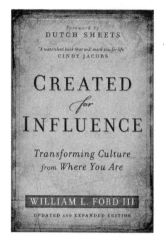

Now revised and expanded, *Created for Influence* shows how you can transform culture from right where you are. Sustained prayer can release influence everywhere—in your own home as well as the highest places of government. This revolutionary book is calling you from a spot on the sidelines to a position on the front lines. It's for everyone ready to change the world around them.

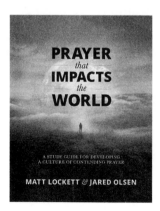

In *Prayer that Impacts the World*, Matt Lockett reveals strategies for change proven effective over many years of prayer and grounded solidly in God's Word. This practical study guide will lead you step-by-step into a deeper walk of prayer with Jesus, learning grace for fasting, cultivating true community, and living out your mission in light of eternity.